to the pedagogic periphery

residentialism
a suburban archipelago

lina malfona

From 2010 onwards, Lina Malfona together with MPA (Malfona Petrini Architecture) and thanks to the support of structural engineer Tommaso Malfona has been designing and building an archipelago of suburban residences in the countryside north of Rome, which is also the location of their home-studio. This experimental residence has become a point of reference for the design of an innovative housing typology, an ultra-residential villa as a place to experience private as well as public life.

This book deals with an open and expanding project, which engages in dialogue with the countryside separatist geography. It tells the story of the making of a COMMUNITY, which occurred hand-in-hand with the building of an archipelago of suburban residences, which reaffirm the value of the countryside within a technological and digital society.

The first book I published about my work, *Building the Landscape. Residential Pavilions in the Roman Countryside*, was a 'typological tale' based on the archetype of the 'residential pavilion', research about form, language, and authorship. This latest book absorbs and expands my previous ideas. It can be defined as a 'PLANIMETRIC STORY' focusing on the archetype of the '*ultra-residential* archipelago', a book about practicing architecture, building communities and shaping forms of belonging.

contents

1. assumptions

Lina Malfona, *A Dwelling*, 2019.

they are homes   pippo ciorra

The trap

The task given me by Lina Malfona is not as simple as it might appear. At first glance, it would seem to be nothing other than the usual work of an architect writing a critical essay on the work of a group of designers. One might imagine this to be all the easier since it concerns gifted designers responsible – despite their relative youth – for a consistent and conspicuous series of buildings that offers more than enough material to satisfy the cupidity and curiosity of the critic.

As it happens, well hidden amongst the houses of Formello lies a more ambitious challenge: the intention of incorporating an external critical gaze into a text that already goes well beyond a simple collection of projects, presented rather as an autonomous theoretical reflection, with one's own work as the starting point. The writer is thus invited to participate in a three-layered product: the critic's review of the project, the monographic presentation of the author's work, and finally the author's own theoretical position strategically placed within the projects. It's a little trap, but one worth falling into, as it seems an excellent opportunity to explore the empathy I feel towards MPA's work, quite rare in the panorama of young, and less young, Italian architecture.

Works

The houses created by the MPA firm in the area of Formello, north of Rome (*Upstate Rome*), are interesting not only for their intrinsic quality of design and execution, but also because they evoke a series of more general *themes*, well rooted both in disciplinary debate and in global discussion on the rapport between architecture, urban planning, and society in our times. The first, the subject of renewed discussion in recent years and now all-absorbing thanks to the pandemic, is obviously the theme of the **NON-collective house**. In the 1990s, thanks to studies by Bernardo Secchi and many others, we saw the sun begin to set on the Manichean vision of *collective residence* as the sole form of habitat ideologically acceptable to enlightened, progressive architects respectful of the city. Thanks to the investigations of a new generation of urban planners, architects and photographers (especially photographers) on the Lombard-Veneto axis or along the Adriatic spine, we slowly began to recognise the existence of millions of single-family homes that constituted the skeletal structure of "diversely urban" life in the country. These houses had nothing to do with the typology of the upper-class villa and were essentially designed (and often built) by the families who live(d) in them.

15

As a result of that elaboration and of thousands of research projects, publications, and conferences on the "diffuse city", the traditional hierarchy of values assigned to modes of living was slowly called into question: proper, democratic, and public-oriented collective living in (and around) the city versus the hardships of the periphery. Diffuse living was seen as selfish, tending toward the asocial, enslaved to American suburban modes and means of communication, too easily invoking the idea of introversion and individualism as false reactions to the power of capitalist societies. The architectonic nihilism that gives form to the diffuse city seemed then to be the proper measure of the aesthetic damnation of this building format.

What has happened in our cities and in our lives in recent years has made it evident to all that this hierarchy of values is no longer applicable. The way in which messages, powers, relationships, and transactions are distributed today between real space and immaterial space in fact renders insufficient the old symbolic topology that identified urban values with political and social ones – high in the centre, fragile in the periphery, regressive in the countryside. Then the pandemic further accelerated the break with traditional constructs and positions of the city versus the non-city. Some architects pushed their conclusions a bit too far, declaring "the end of the city" in favour of the "burgs" and the return to small-scale communities. Their statements are nonetheless useful for understanding how to begin considering the environmental system in its entirety, englobing urban fabrics and diffuse living (each in its thousand meanings) in search of a complete environmental equilibrium. Lina Malfona and MPA, though, are perhaps the only ones to have accepted these new living conditions as a true starting point and theoretical assumption of their work, skilfully undertaking an experiment of collective/individual design previously unknown in Italy.

The second "noble" theme in MPA's architectonic narrative, stretched between Rome and Lake Bracciano, is the "series". It is a specialty in design quite popular in international and (obviously) North American contexts, but is also tied to specific Italian experiences or particular cases. Overseas canonical references abound, from the Case Study House Program in Los Angeles to the residential sequences of Eisenman, Meier, Gehry, Murcutt and many others. But we must not forget certain interesting experiments in Europe and Italy, such as those connected to great expositive events— the Weissenhof project in Stuttgart as well as the Triennale of Milan – to architectonic contexts more accustomed to the single-family house. As mentioned above, it is difficult to ignore some residential sequences by The New York Five, considering the prevalence of white and Malfona's declared interest in a mannerist approach to language.

Another strong assonance, a *naughty thought* not to be erased by us Italians and Romans, is certainly that of Mario Ridolfi. Rooted in the urban and suburban areas of Terni and in the Nera River basin, Ridolfi held great affection for social context, as well as a preference for materials of local construction. Ridolfi was a "communist architect" for historiography and for the world, but author of some of the most beautiful single-family homes of the period for the people of Terni.

MPA has the great fortune, the perseverance and the courage to explore this particular way of producing architecture. It is a very specific modality, whose typological repetition permits us to take certain contextual elements for granted, exalting the authorial aspect (intended precisely as the author describes it in her *assumptions*) and the philosophical and artistic content of the work. Closed in a dimension and in a series of assigned narrative rules, as in a film, a book, a portrait, or a photograph, the *sequence of homes* allows the author to progressively refine her instruments and the critic to follow and understand her evolution with perfect clarity. This is certainly an evident characteristic of MPA's work, halfway between a condition and a choice that has nonetheless permitted their expressive arsenal to develop in a clear and harmonious way.

When she describes them, Malfona tends to divide her groups of houses into *villages* when they are collected in bunches, favouring neighbourly rapport, and into *archipelagos* when they are more spread out in order to take advantage of the space afforded by the diffuse city, constructing a more individual rapport with the landscape. Of course, the way that the author discusses these things in the book makes it clear that she considers her houses a piece of the **city**. The low density, the distance from the medieval centre of Formello and from metropolitan Rome are not enough to convince Malfona that the houses presented here are not, in their own way, the city. Neither better nor worse than the dense city.

As mentioned above, we are seeing such a reassessment of processes and values that we can no longer allow ourselves to consider the relationship between dense city and countryside, residence and workplace, private life and social life, in the same terms as those of the entire 20th century. The people who live in these MPA houses generally work in Rome and split the public part of their existence between Rome and the place where they live. It is a particularity of these developments that the home itself expands into "internal public spaces": places for work, for gatherings, for collective recreation, for production, that make each of these residences a part of the collective life of the community, regardless of its collocation within the urban blueprint. "...[T]he residential program alone," Malfona writes, "does not satisfy the aspirations of those families who have recently chosen to move to the suburbs. For this reason, each of the houses that my office has built in the countryside hosts a sort of collective program, in addition to the residential one. Thanks to the double program, this archipelago of homes triggers an environmental transformation process, which reactivates the sleepy suburbs." I'll add that it contributes to a discussion of what we mean today by city, or better, as relationship between collective space and individual space.

The firm, but especially Malfona, has a clear interest in questions of expression and "of **language**". Passion is very evident and is tied to the original interests and education of the author and of the group: the controlled excess of Franco Purini, Roman Rationalism, hyper-modernist *mannerism* – which is evoked several times – in meaning of late and very late modernity as passed down to us by Colin Rowe. Most interesting, in the text and in the sequence of the projects, is the expressive evolution that we can follow in the tight sequence of structures. The continuity of scale, function, and context already addressed becomes an essential palimpsest for putting MPA's growth into focus. In discussing the earliest houses, which were born of an almost ferocious attraction to the "pavilion" typology, the author lingers on certain points connected to specific structural solutions. This probably serves to redeem the geometric and functional essentiality of the type, providing the client with enough expressive and spatial richness to make up for the lack of luxury in materials and details. We see this quite well, for instance, in the restless forms of the three "Windows on the River" houses, completed in 2017, and in other less recent projects.

As the MPA series expands into the countryside north of Rome, the houses become less and less dependent on the performance of language and exhibited complexity, discovering other and even more interesting tones: the apparent planimetric clarity in relation to the complexity of the ground, the use of colour, the insistence on the programme's hybrid nature, the ever greater relationship of continuity with the landscape. One could say that Malfona and her colleagues are accompanying the architecture of the house on its journey outside the 20th-century canon, rigidly marked by the opposition of the richness of a villa to the dimensions of a small house, ferrying it into our own times. Now the single-family home is fundamentally displaced fragment of the city, "the post-urban place where drones land", as essential as an urban residence can be, where the inhabitant can work, produce, relax with family or friends, isolate, live in contact with the land. The abundance of meanings goes along with the conquest of a more formal essentiality, as though the space simply must be available for this plurality of uses. The design that symbolises this precocious maturity is likely the home-office "La Villa", where planimetric articulation, relation to the ground, colours, and building rhythms are all pushed to the highest intensity.

Theories

I will close with a note on the specific nature of this book, both monograph and **theoretical text**. Since the 1990s, the category of the monograph accompanied by external critical text has been in crisis. Since the publication of **S,M, L, XL** (Koolhaas & Mau, 1995), architects, and especially the most influential ones, have decided that they do not want critical monographs, preferring to "write" their books themselves. Or better, more than writing, they want to transform the book into a hypertext of communication and propaganda with a high capacity for penetration, perhaps even calling in a dazzling graphic designers rather than an authoritative critic. The intended audience of publications was not first and foremost those in the field but rather a broader one, from the media world to prospective clients to the myriad of students and followers ready to consider the book more as a cult object than as a text.

Malfona attempts a complex operation: on the one hand, the recovery, via her texts, of a good portion of the theoretical weight that the "masters" once gave the books that contained their designs and buildings; on the other, continuing to consider the book as a work unto itself, in which images, texts, graphics, and drawings are rigorously inserted into an autonomous communicative project. The result is achieved via an inversion: contrary to what usually happens in a monograph, here the sequence of chapters follows the succession of themes while the projects are used as illustrations of the author's theoretical arguments. This choice reveals the author's academic identity, her international experiences, and the compulsion to provoke a discussion on architecture that is not guided solely by external agents (environment, technology, sociology). The text certainly achieves its aim, pushing us to discuss architecture and the city in the terms of the author's own choosing.

1. assumptions

Lina Malfona, *A Dwelling*, 2019.

1. Thomas S. Eliot, *Selected Essays, 1917-1932*, New York: Harcourt, Brace and Co., 1932, 18.

2. Robert Venturi, *Note to the Second Edition*, id., *Complexity and Contradiction in Architecture*, New York: The Museum of Modern Art, 1977, 15.

3. Michel Foucault, *What Is an Author?* (1969), James D. Faubion (ed.), *Esthetics, Method, and Epistemology (Essential Works of Foucault, 1954-1984)*, New York: The New Press, 1998, 221.

4. August Heckscher, *The Public Happiness*, New York: Atheneum Publishers, 1962, 102.

I mantain that the criticism employed by a trained and skilled writer on his own work is the most vital, the highest kind of criticism.[1]

I consider architecture to be the result of a theoretical, physical and spiritual labor.

I believe in the tectonic value of architecture and in its useful beauty.

I regard drawing as an autonomous and integral practice, as a parallel to design.

Nowadays, architects' hands and eyes cut across many disciplines. I support that architects can use their disciplinary knowledge as a lens to read the world of art and media, scientific and technological thought, and the social, cultural, and geopolitical realms. Nevertheless, architects are still called to face architecture as the essential human habitat. Being an architect today means creating multiple partitions in your brains.

Should an artist go all the way with his or her philosophies?[2]

To be an architect means continuing to work as an author while discussing, reconsidering and editing the condition of being an author.

In short, it is a matter of depriving the subject of its role as originator, and of analyzing the subject as a variable and complex function of discourse.[3]

The movement from a view of life as essentially simple and orderly to a view of life as complex and ironic is what every individual passes through in becoming mature.[4]

Architects have to continuously revise the social implications of concepts such as belonging and identity within the process of creating new communities.

By authorship I mean the crystallization of the designer's political and social action in architectural form, an effort that allows the author's hand to be glimpsed only in filigree.

2. *upstate rome*
a suburban* atlas

* The concept of "suburban" reveals a new residential paradigm that challenges central living and highlights new technological, social and economic possibilities for peripheral areas, intended as the place for autonomous thought. I decided to use the term "suburban" instead of "exurban" because it has strongly Italian connotations. Suburban refers to areas located on the edge of a city (*suburbium*) and consisting mainly of homes, where people who work in the city often live. This term recalls the Roman suburban villa and assumes the presence of a city to which suburban living refers, which in this case is Rome.

upstate rome

Upstate Rome is a state of mind. It is a condition, not just a physical place. It is the Rome of commuters, who accept an inconvenient travelling in exchange for a range of advantages, such as a house surrounded by a pleasant landscape, away from the city's pollution. These characteristics cannot but call to mind those commuter towns surrounding other metropolitan areas, especially the North American ones, where many well-off families prefer to make their dream come true in nearby suburbs rather than in the cities themselves. Usually these families prefer to move straight to the countryside because here they can live in a larger house, with a garden and pool. This leap out of the city is one of the main troubles of Rome that, no longer capable of taking care of its suburbs, is losing its last urban ring. *Upstate Rome* is analogous to Upstate New York and shows the sameness of suburban conditions, where isolation is the main issue. «This residential silence—Gianni Celati wrote in his book "Verso la foce"—is completely different from that of the open space».

MPA, *Finestre sul fiume*, 2017. Aerial view.

geometra style

Vernacular traits of the Roman countryside have been hybridized with portable identities, made of experiences, rituals and social practices, caused by migrations and exchanges. In particular, this territory shows a folkloristic vernacular, the so called "*geometra* style", which refers to the building anarchy of spontaneous and abusive homes. According to the moviemaker Giacomo Gili, the "*geometra* style" shows a *joie de vivre*, expressed by the use of color, liveliness, bricolage as a construction technique, and typically Italian fun. Although architecture culture has not generally been concerned with this whimsical anarchy, it is possible to look at this phenomenon from the perspective of an anthropologist, taking into account the work of Ed Rusha (*Twenty Six Gasoline Stations*, 1963), Hilla and Bernd Becher (*Industriebauten 1830-1930*), and Giuseppe Pagano (*Architettura Rurale Italiana*, 1936). These studies on vernacular landscape have shown how the construction of a language can take advantage of the specificity of places, perhaps capturing their spontaneity and liveliness.

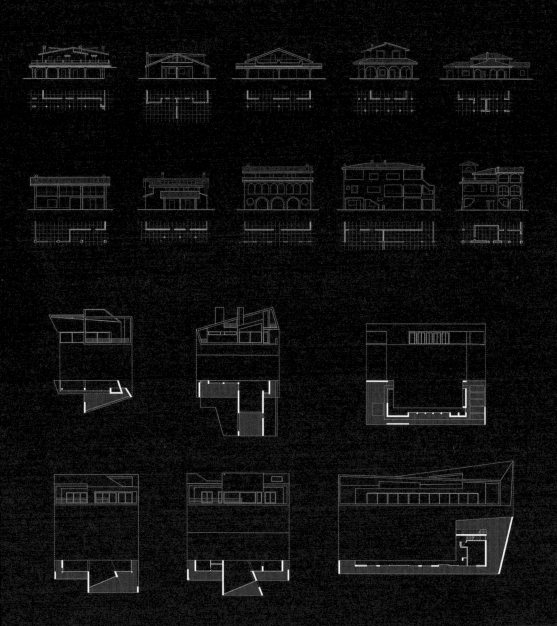

Yuzhen Zhang, Lina Malfona, *Vernacular | Contemporary*, 2018.
Comparison between vernacular houses in Formello and MPA buildings.

archipelago

The archipelago is a landscape form that represents the refusal of the idea of centrality. It discloses the very act of breaking up, dismembering and demolishing any center. Over time this form has been used as an urban metaphor, conveying the idyllic vision of a city whose neighborhoods are surrounded by greenery (Oswald Mathias Ungers, *The city in the city, Berlin: A green archipelago*, 1977). The constellation of houses that my office built in the countryside north of Rome, in Formello, has been designed selecting from the city certain settlement strategies to be applied to the countryside. In this process, the archipelago emerged as one of the most appropriate design tools to overcome the separatist geography of the countryside. The drawing on the right shows in a single frame all the houses designed in Formello. Over time, this archipelago—made up of people, pets, plants, homes, and technological gizmos—has become a romantic and evocative «garden of wande ring» for people who relocate fragments of their identity from one place to the other.

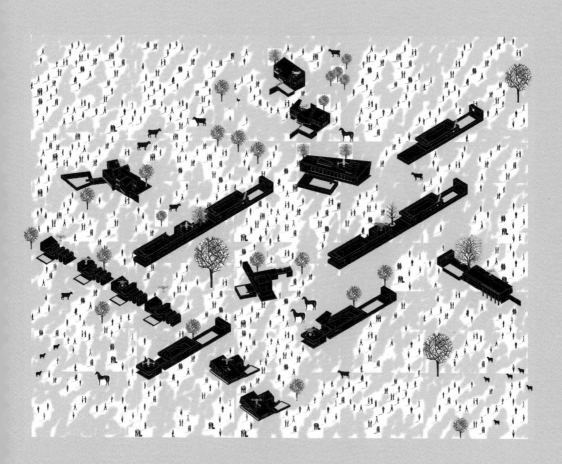

Lina Malfona, *Archipelago*, 2018.

objects of affection

In the country and suburban areas you can find some peculiar objects of affection: fragments of the past used as a quotation; farm tools restored and exhibited in farmhouses; garages, rooms and outbuildings located in the garden where objects of affection are kept; large hay bales designing the landscape. You can even find surreal objects like the cylinder of an air conditioner that comes out of the windows like a proboscis.

Agricultural tool, air conditioner duct and hay bales in Formello.

surrealism in the suburbs

Images of saints used as murals or embedded as tabernacles on blind facades of residential buildings; overbearing billboards placed on street corners; *trompe l'oeil* windows placed in unlikely interiors; two-tone houses emerging from the bushes. The countryside is made up of displaced objects that diverge from their context of belonging.

Saint looking out from the balcony; *trompe l'oeil* window in a suburban bakery; two-tone semi-detached house in Formello.

continuous interior

In the suburbs home is ubiquitous. Shops and stores are located in buildings formerly designed to be homes. In order to create domesticity, even cafes and restaurants—located into recycled warehouses and industrial buildings—are set up like homes. Anyone can walk into and feel at home because the interior space is made up of the same elements that you find in your own home. This 'home style' which prevails in shopping malls and collective facilities promotes the concept of 'continuous interiors', which means making anonymous places domestic. Floors covered with false parquet and walls covered with false stone are used to 'domesticate' these places, which are frequently completed by artificial plants and the flame from a bioethanol fireplace.

Café and restaurant located in a warehouse in Formello.

rituals

The porch represents the public dimension of a private interior. It is the place where the house's public life takes place. Like the veranda and the pergola, the porch is an icon for suburban family. Baptisms, anniversaries and family celebrations have been always performed under the porch and still today it is a protected place from the humidity of the irrigated countryside, used for meetings and dinners with friends.

MPA, *The Aqueduct*, 2018.

pool

In the last scene of the movie *C'eravamo tanto amati*, Vittorio Gassman jumps off a diving board and into the pool at his villa in Olgiata, northern Rome. The film director Ettore Scola sees the villa in Olgiata with the pool, surrounded by laurel hedges, as the status symbol of the wealthy Roman entrepreneurs who have been residing in the luxurious suburbs north of Rome since the seventies. Today the stereotyped villa with its accompanying pool is no longer a symbol of the Roman upper class, who lives in the city center, but it is the prerogative of a middle professional class, who takes a shelter into the small, maze-like and sometimes unpaved roads of Formello.

ultra-residential

In the suburbs the home is the place where people prefer
to gather, the privileged place where conversations
with neighbors and Sunday meetings take place. But
the residential program alone does not satisfy the
aspirations of those families who recently chose to
move to the suburbs. For this reason, each of the houses
that my office built in the countryside hosts a collective
program, in addition to the residential one. Thanks to the
double program, this archipelago of homes triggers an
environmental transformation process, which reactivates
the sleepy suburbs.

MPA, *La casa sul bosco*, 2019. Living area.

public home

According to the Brazilian master Paulo Mendes da Rocha, there is no private space but only different degrees of public space.

Today this insightful thought can be seen as an old prophecy. The loss of domestic intimacy following the current transformation of the home into a public place—the background of remote working and conference calls—leads us to rethink the interior space of our homes. Since cameras have forcefully invaded our privacy, it may be necessary to protect our space or to show only parts of it, to cut it out or set it up according to the circumstances. This transformation of the domestic world into a performative environment emphasizes another ongoing trend in the Instagram age, the all-encompassing dimensions of the *mise-en-scène*, a condition that is already affecting our habits and our ways of life.

MPA, *La Villa*, 2020. The house transformation into a movie set.

neighbourhood

Springfield is a fictional town in the sitcom *The Simpsons*.
This toponym is very common in America, Springfield
is indeed intended to represent any town in the U.S.
On closer inspection, Springfield epitomizes the whole
suburban America, a vast territory whose sameness means
that the same flag flies from every house. Springfield is
also a complete universe, the village in which every human
event takes place. Nevertheless its geography is flexible
and changing to address every plot variation.

The town of Springfield

village

The village is a settlement condition as well as a planning strategy, characterized by a specific program—work, leisure, tourism, health—and based on a strong residential presence. Villages are usually made up of villas, houses or residential pavilions and equipped with gardens, squares and collective amenities. The village is a place for dreamers like Marc Chagall painting, *The Joy of the Village* (1957).
In case of pandemics, the constellation of houses that MPA built in the countryside north of Rome might be temporarily isolated and quarantined, since the residential program is enhanced by a series of collective facilities, incorporated inside the houses. This archipelago might thus easily be turned into a self-sufficient and protected environment, an integral village.

Lina Malfona, *The Village*, 2019

3. overturning suburbia separatist geography

Thus, for me, a liberative promise for the future resides in an agonistic architecture of the periphery as opposed to the subtle nonjudgmental conformism of ruling taste emanating from the centre.

Kenneth Frampton, "Verso un'architettura agonistica|Towards an Agonistic Architecture", *Domus*, no. 972, September 2013, 1-8.

Gated communities, social pods, garden cities, campsites, holiday and temporary settlements, luxury suburban communities, company towns, renewed *kibbutz*... Today suburban living can alternately be seen as a nostalgic myth, a dystopian habitat, or a sanctuary as a protection from wars, climate changes or pandemics. From the rhetoric of the global village to the recent rediscovery of the intrinsic values of neighborhood, suburban living fulfills the desire for a new environment for experiencing new models of social engagement. Since the recent possibilities offered by remote working make the countryside an ideal environment as well as a real opportunity, suburban living emerges as one of the most privileged conditions.

This book tells the story of an archipelago of villas designed long before the novel coronavirus appeared, when a high number of families started to get away from cities toward the countryside of an unpredicted 'upstate Rome'. Considering the large number of families involved in this process, this voluntary relocation can be viewed as a social and economic phenomenon. However, given the timeless attractive power of cities, it was also an anti-urban, therefore unexpected, phenomenon, foretelling what would have happened in the future, in our present. These families accepted an enormously inconvenient commute in exchange for a range of advantages: a low-cost and large-sized home surrounded by a pleasant landscape, away from the city's pollution and located in an environment that meets their needs and expectations. In the suburbs they live a lifestyle that, while comfortable, is also devoted to concentration and a kind of enlightened isolation based on total immersion in the landscape. These assets are not mere compensations for the distance from the urban center but are viewed rather as an antidote to the urban disease.

But if isolation from the city is synonymous with a voluntary rejection of urban lifestyle it also reinforces a kind of elitist culture. This two-sided nature of suburban living was the starting point for the design process.

The suburban villa represents an escape from the city. Consider the Roman villa, which came to be used for enjoying country life or as a place for intellectual pursuits. Pliny the Younger wrote of the villa as a place of quietness and intellectual well-being, extended into the landscape almost by germination, through its long arms, paths,

Roman Landscape.
Old farmhouse (*casale*) along the ancient Via Francigena,
between Formello and Isola Farnese.

pergolas and cryptoporticoes, somehow anticipating the typology of the house made up of pavilions. Pliny himself owned two suburban villas: the one located in the Apennines, *Villa in Tuscis*, and the other on the Tyrrhenian coast not far from Rome, the *Laurentinum*. Only Pliny's description and a few ruins of this latter villa remain, but many architects, including Karl Friedrich Schinkel, tried to make reconstruction drawings of this enigmatic villa, influenced by these descriptions. The architect Leon Krier was the author of one of the most bizarre and visionary reconstructions of the *Laurentinum*, drawing this house as a fortified garrison, suspended between the image of Villa Malaparte in Capri and Pius II Piccolomini's city plan, a postmodern mash-up of an acropolis, a medieval village and a Renaissance city. And it was still Krier who sketched out a very careful outline of the suburban villa, a residence intended as a 'villa-ge' made up of a set of private and public buildings:

This villa is not a closed world, it is not a monastery, or a royal palace. It is an ensemble of buildings which serve very diverse functions; sometimes strictly private, sometimes very public. [...] Through his text, Pliny encouraged me to conceive his villa as a great number of separate buildings. This villa-ge does not have to ward off pirates.[1]

1. Leon Krier, "Houses, Palaces, Cities," *Architectural Design* 54, no. 7/8, 1984, 121.

Through these words, Krier highlighted the dual nature of the suburban villa, a protected world but also an open organism, a private and contemporary public residence, a hermitage and a meeting place, a control center as well as a hub to connect sprawling suburbs. Another Roman villa, the Neronian Domus Aurea expresses a further characteristic of suburban living: it was a productive villa, a luxurious home designed as a laboratory for experimenting with innovative architectural and artistic solutions, a creative cabinet that testifies to the penetration of different cultures, including especially the Hellenic one, within Roman culture. Many Roman villas were large enough to absorb residential and productive programs within them. Often these programs were separated from each other and over time this functional division gave life to a peculiar house typology, made up of two or more blocks, each of which generally opened on a courtyard, as in the villa of San Rocco in Francolise and in that of Settefinestre, near Orbetello. In other Roman villas, however, residential, working, productive and commercial programs were all concentrated in a single

MPA, *The Aqueduct*, 2018.
Facade of the small pavilion flanking the pool.
It hosts an outdoor kitchen and a changing room
on the ground floor, and a tool room in the basement.

Farmhouse in Formello

2. Cf James S. Ackerman, *The villa. Form and Ideology of Country Houses*, Princeton: Princeton University Press, 1990, chapters I,II, III.

3. The term 'domestication', comes from the Latin *domesticus*, or 'belonging to the house'. I am evidently misusing the term 'domestication' to explain the current practice of incorporating one's workplace and social life into the home.
The reader is asked to consider the increase in remote working during the current pandemic, as well as the practice of starting business within one's own home, which is very common in the suburbs.

large residence, without any separation into functional areas. In the villa in Boscoreale near Pompeii, for example, stables, rooms for pressing grapes, fermenting yard, servants' quarters, rooms for the family, oil-pressing rooms, oven and baths were thickened together without a clear interior division.[2] Productive and residential programs came to be integrated programs, anticipating not just the family business' domesticity, which is a typical Italian practice, but also the hybridization of work and residential programs, which is so frequent today.

Taking these and other ancient dwellings as references and reading their main features, the process of construction of single-family houses in the countryside north of Rome helped develop a new idea of suburban sociality, which involves a private as well as civic dimension. Also, in the framework of an ongoing process of 'domestication'[3] —when business and social interaction take place within the home, thanks to remote communication—this project outlines an innovative house typology, an 'ultra-residential villa' which combines both the private and public realms. It introduces associated, connected, incorporated or complementary programs into the residence, bringing not just business but also collective life at home to contrast the separatist geography of suburbia.

In *Upstate Rome*, privacy means security and it is intended as a way to control. Here, home is the legacy of the vernacular *casale*, an enclave of nourishment, a bulwark whose origins date back to the Middle Ages. Towering laurel hedges, separating villas with pools from the street, are the status symbol of Roman entrepreneurs, professionals and artists residing in the suburbs north of the city since the seventies. However, in the suburbs, home is also the place where people usually gather, where they start their own practice, the privileged place where conversations with neighbors, friendly meetings as well as formal dinners take place. Taking these social practices into account, a series of residences located a short distance from each other have been created from 2010 onwards. Each villa has a non-residential complement, linked to the users' work and interests. This collective area allows the residence to be used as a private-collective property, in order to reduce the dormitory effect and increase the number of amenities in the suburbs. The final result has been an open and expanding project, an archipelago of 'ultra-residential' villas, including a bnb house, a house with a

MPA houses in Formello.

showroom, a home-studio and a home restaurant. This innovation, together with the new spirit of the sharing economy and the spread of smart working, encouraged many families to move towards the countryside, where they could reinvent their own structure and living space. Also, due to the current economic instability and the more and more frequent family contraction,[4] people decided to open their home to other guests to experiment with new forms of coexistence, which often determine a transformation of the house into a productive activity, an income-generating property.

The house transformations and its typological hybridization still need to be explored in the countryside, where *ultra-residential* programs could provide further opportunities for mending the existing built fabric and social relationships.

Thanks to this double program, in case of pandemics the archipelago built in the Roman countryside could be easily isolated, quarantined and turned into a self-sufficient village. Nowadays this dystopian scenario cannot be ignored. Also, this design implements a symbiotic relationship between architecture, engineering and digital technologies in order to create low-cost, energy-saving and self-sufficient residencies, almost completely disconnected from any public network. At this point, the overall archipelago can be utterly turned into an offline village.

To summarize the process, this constellation of houses, wich developed from a series of independent design opportunities, over time has became an archipelago of residences. The archipelago as a landscape, territorial and urban condition has emerged as one of the most appropriate design tools, an open, adaptative strategy to build communities endowed with urban values. New programs have been integrated into the exclusively residential one for wich these homes were initially commissioned. These new peograms have turned the early residential constellation into a place where the home gains an eminently social role. Given its flexible settlement structure, this archipelago could also become a closed and protected settlement in case of unfortunate events, a sort of offline village. And since the houses are already equipped with technologies for energy storage, this village—although this is not desirable option—is fully prepared to function autonously.

4. Consider the growing percentage of young citizens who leave their own country for studying and working abroad.

4. building collective individualities

True architecture requires humility (pride), the highest spirit.
[La vera architettura richiede umiltà (orgoglio), spirito altissimo].

Piero Bottoni, "Crociata o torneo della 'casa per tutti'", *Costruzioni-Casabella*, a. XVI, 1943, n. 187

1. Fred Koetter, "The Corporate Villa," *Design Quarterly*, no. 135, 1987, 1-31, 11.

2. Like Jefferson, Wright maintained an agricultural faith that would have replaced the modern city with an expanded version of the provincial town, in which each inhabitant could claim the right to use at least one acre of land. Cf James S. Ackerman, *The villa. Form and Ideology of Country Houses*, ibidem, chapter: "The modern villa: Wright and Le Corbusier."

3. Cf Jean-Luc Nancy, *Essere Singolare Plurale*, Torino: Einaudi 2001 (1st ed. *Être singulier pluriel*, Paris: Éditions Galilée, 1996), 45.

4. Nicolas Bourriaud, *Relational Esthetics*, Dijon: Les presses du réel, 2002 (1st ed. *Esthétique relationnelle*, Dijon: Les presses du reel, 1998), 45-46.

5. Regarding the definition of 'residential pavilion', see: Lina Malfona, *Building the Landscape. Residential Pavilions in the Roman Countryside*, Siracusa: Lettera Ventidue, 35-37.

Thomas Jefferson defined the villa as a place for an ideal suburban society, far from the city's corruption. In the neo-Palladian house he designed for himself in Monticello, he sought the development of a new type of society derived from the model «urbanity without urbanism»[1] —the potential of this model was later recovered by Frank Lloyd Wright through the residences he built in Wisconsin and Arizona.[2] Even today, the design of single-family houses in the countryside—a relatively irrelevant practice from the point of view of the global economy, and in some ways sheltered from those processes that direct building development—can be recognized as a craft whose aim is the creation of places where it is possible to participate in a new idea of sociability.

Focusing on the typology of the single-family house, the project illustrated here will show how in suburban territories the residence is still the generative cell of a community. Therefore the design of single-family houses in the countryside is not a *disurbanist* operation but a proactive action, aimed at building a sense of community. In his essay on the plural condition of existence, the philosopher Jean-Luc Nancy argues that a community is not characterized by the concept of identity but by the idea of sharing, since the ego is not thinkable except in relation to others. The essence of being is properly a co-essence, according to Nancy.[3] Similarly, the curator and art critic Nicolas Bourriaud claims that today any artwork is a relational object, not only a product but essentially a process. It is intended as a cooperative system, as the place of negotiations, ties and coexistences with countless interlocutors:

We no longer try to make progress thanks to conflict and clashes, but by discovering new assemblages, possible relations between distinct units, and by building alliances between different partners. Like social contracts, aesthetic contracts are seen for what they are: no one expects the Golden Age to be ushered in on this earth, and we are quite happy to create modus vivendi that make possible fairer social relations, more dense ways of life, and multiple, fruitful combinations of existence.[4]

The concept of «relational aesthetics» allowed me to conceive of the suburban house as the place where users can live alone but at the same time feel part of a community, the 'residential pavilion' where 'collective individuality' is formed.[5]

Formello, 2019.

Lina Malfona, The town of Formello in the province of Rome.

6. Cf Nicolas Bourriaud, *Inclusioni. Estetica del capitalocene*, Postmedia Books, 2021 (I ed. *Inclusions. Esthétique du capitalocène*, Paris: Presses Universitaires de France, 2020), 12.

7. Regarding the definition of 'collective memory' see: Maurice Halbwachs, *La Mémoire Collective*, Paris: Presses Universitaires de France, 1949; Aldo Rossi, *The Architecture of the City*, Cambridge MA: The MIT Press, 1982 (1st ed. *L'architettura della città*, Padova: Marsilio, 1966), 130.

8. Richard Sennett explained the effects of a different type of 'social pod' by analyzing the Jews' confinement in the Venetian Ghetto. The American sociologist argued that the Jews' forced seclusion contributed to both the development of a sense of mutual solidarity and the construction of collective identity. Cf Richard Sennett, *Lo straniero*, Milano: Feltrinelli, 2014 (1st ed. *The Foreigner: Two Essays on Exile*, Kendal: Notting Hill Editions, 2011), 34-35.

In the last ten years, my colleagues and I have been designing and building an archipelago of villas located a short distance from each other in Formello, a small town in the countryside north of Rome. Since 2008, MPA has carried out an architectural as well as a social experiment, creating a continuous workshop, open to students, manufacturers and users, which fosters unusual and creative ties. From the beginning, the design process was independent from political control and it rather involved new forms of political engagement, establishing a negotiated code between clients and architects, supporting the creation of agreements between the owners of building lands, and proposing the revision of the building regulation of this small town. If it is true that the powers-that-be tolerate the presence of art only in the peripheral, marginal areas of the system, since it does not represent a direct threat here[6], then the peripheral can unexpectedly reveal itself as a privileged condition, one in which it is possible to enjoy a certain autonomy of thought. This is not the meager consolation for suburban thinkers but a growing awareness. The current state of this project is a collection of more than twelve experimental architectures, which contribute to defining an adaptive, relational and multifaceted community, one might say a resilient community without common roots, open to welcoming new components.

Conversely Formello—the small town where I started my practice—epitomizes the idea of a traditional community, whose inhabitants share spaces, customs and a collective memory.[7] In the past, these settlements fostered the building of a collective identity, which implies ethnic or religious affinities.[8] Overcoming this concept, Jean-Luc Nancy claims that a community is no longer characterized by the concept of identity but more properly by the concept of coexistence.

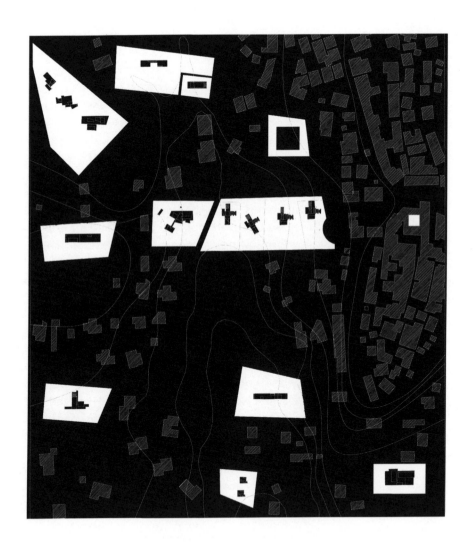

Lina Malfona, *Residential archipelago in* Upstate Rome, 2020.

Community is not a gathering of individuals, posterior to the elaboration of individuality, for individuality as such can be given only within such a gathering [...] Community and communication are constitutive of individuality, rather than the reverse, and individuality is perhaps, in the final analysis, only a boundary of community.[9]

9. Jean-Luc Nancy, *The Birth to Presence*, Stanford: Stanford University Press, 1993, 153-154.

10. This theory has been deployed as a response to Gayatri Chakravorty Spivak's 'strategic essentialism'. It refers to the consequences of her thought on claiming local identity in a de-westernizing perspective. Cf Nicolas Bourriaud, *Radicant: Pour une esthétique de la globalisation*, New York: Lukas & Steinberg, 2009, 26-34; Gayatri Chakravorty Spivak, *In Other Words*, New York: Methuen, 1987, 205.

11. Nicolas Bourriaud, *The Radicant*, New York: Lukas & Steinberg, 2009, 56.

Today building communities means questioning the conditions of coexisting and belonging. Coexisting might not imply belonging to a place. Belonging instead means rooting in a specific place, and it is not an immediate process but rather a natural and gradual adaptation. According to Nicolas Bourriaud, postcolonial theories have failed in considering individuals as definitively assigned to their local and cultural roots. Today individuals tend to move through different places and take on multiple identities. Continuing to focus on belonging, and excluding relocation processes, postcolonial thinking promotes an idea of ethnic roots that stop any social development. Thus, postcolonial theories, which were supposed to struggle against alienation, instead assign the individual a single place, a single identity, and a single language, definitively blocking them in a symbolic home detention, that of essentialist theme parks. On the contrary, Bourriaud's thought overcomes the idea of taking roots through «radicant» thought:[10]

Radicant thought is not a defense of voluntary amnesia but of relativism, unsubscription, and departure. Its true adversaries are neither tradition nor local cultures, but confinement within readymade cultural schemata—when habits become forms—and enrootedness, as soon as it becomes a rhetoric of identity. It is not a matter of rejecting one's heritage but rather of learning to squander it, of plotting the line along which one will then carry this baggage in order to scatter and invest its contents.[11]

The process leading to the construction of a constellation of houses in the landscape was a sort of training manual, which never relied on consolidated ideas but always questioned every apparent truth, every prejudicial belief in search of deeper architectural and settlement paradigms. Over time, it became clear that the use of a specific architectural language made these homes similar and that the same style has played a decisive role in developing a feeling of belonging, in addition to simple coexistence.

on the next page
MPA, *La Villa*, 2014-. Ultra-residential use of the house as a set.

Country Scenes, 2019.
Fences, signals, gates, pools, homes

As an author, what appeared as an unexpected but considerable discovery to me was that an individual syntax is able to shape a collective sense of community. If it is true that architecture is the art of creating useful forms, the architect is a form-giver, equipped with an artistic and contemporarily a technical-scientific knowledge, and endowed with a creative power. Today this power is inappropriately considered as an authoritarian and imposing practice, or in the worst cases as a neo-colonialist act, while architects can responsibly use their influence to improve the living conditions of people and places, using beauty as a cure. Nancy and Bourriaud's reflections on overcoming the traditional concept of community also offered the opportunity to rethink the concept of authorship in architecture. The authorial model is indeed not an authoritative model; on the contrary it implies civic responsibility and stimulates the creation of a strong synergy between author and users, a relationship in which the role of the architect, however, cannot be secondary. By authorship I mean the crystallization of the designer's political and social action in architectural form, an effort that allows the author's hand to be glimpsed, even if only in filigree. The shift of creative tension from the production of objects to the making of communities—read as adaptive and resilient systems—made it possible to better understand how research on architectural form can induce new models of sociality and new forms of coexistence. These first considerations lead to a tentative definition of architecture as the art of creating innovative and useful forms, which on the one hand creates intimacy and on the other stimulates sociality.

Usually, those who relocate to the Roman countryside are looking for a peaceful and healthful place to live quietly. This detached behavior subverts the traditional concept of community, since these individuals have no common roots and prefer to live perched on the hills, instead of in the village. Over time, this archipelago—made up of people, pets, plants, homes, and technological gizmos[12]—became a romantic and evocative «garden of wandering»[13] for people who usually relocate fragments of their identity from one place to the other. Vernacular traits come to be continually hybridized with portable identities, made of experiences, rituals and social practices. In this way, a community of foreigners, or better 'new locals', has subverted the traditional concept of belonging. After the construction of the first houses and as soon as the idea of an archipelago started to emerge, my role was

12. Among the most popular technological devices in suburban environments we cannot fail to mention alarms, sensors, cameras and anti-theft devices, brushcutters, lawnmowers, sprayers and robots for cleaning swimming pools.

13. Cf Michel Serres, *Atlas*, Paris: Éditions Julliard, 1994.

Lina Malfona, *Lo spazio dell'attesa*, 2014.

14. Cf Zygmunt Bauman, *Liquid Life*, Cambridge UK, Malden MA: Polity Press, 2005.

15. A remarkable as well as parallel experience is that of Stan Allen in in the Hudson Valley, north of New York. Cf Stan Allen, with contributions by Helen Thomas and Jesús Vassallo, *Situated Objects. Buildings and Projects by Stan Allen, Photographs by Scott Benedict*, Zürich: Park Books, 2020.

not only to support this process but also to try to guide it by building a new idea of community. As an architect, I was responsible for harmonizing the dialectics between settlement ratio, architectural form, and social programs. As an author, I had to reconsider the social implications of concepts such as 'belonging' and 'identity' within the process of creating new communities. In light of my personal experience as a foreigner and in light of the testimony provided by our clients, I found it necessary to combine the practice of taking roots with the experience of moving across, in a way to promote an idea of coexistence that invests in differences, by identifying them as further possibilities. Thus, the construction of collective individuality does not address the search for common grounds but rather the reception of what is different and as such can enrich local identity.

What I immediately learned from this design experience is that people who landed in the Roman countryside from abroad are in love with this landscape but refuse to be identified by vernacular homes. They prefer a modern design, characterized by a certain degree of lightness, which is also a metaphor for their flexible, temporary and 'liquid' lifestyle.[14] Even if they do not create a community in a traditional sense, the architecture where they chose to dwell makes them similar, connected: this architecture identifies them, creating another kind of community.[15] This parallel Formello is made up of buildings that protect you and contemporarily allow you to look far away. They are characterized by a central core and an envelope; the coexistence of both represents the relationship between intimacy and sociality. These themes are articulated through the interpretation of the wishes and ambitions of these 'new locals' mediated by the architect's design philosophy.
In particular, the concept of a house which is developed around two elements, the core and the envelope, characterized the first phase of my work. In this period, my office created seven white houses, whose complex geometries interpreted the landscape morphology. The houses built in this first period supply a reading of the suburban villa as a 'residential pavilion', a structure with an enveloping lightness, conceived as both a house and a tent. The term 'pavilion' has bourgeois origins: it emerged as a house for pleasurable or health-related purposes just outside the city, or sometimes as a country house. In the seventeenth century, the word 'pavilion' began to be used to indicate a small, elegant and isolated construction located in the gardens and grounds of the

vilion' began to be used to indicate a small, elegant and isolated construction located in the gardens and grounds of the aristocracy; later on, the term was used to describe an isolated building erected in a public space. Nowadays the term 'pavilion' has lost its domestic dimension and it is commonly used to describe a light, dismountable structure at a market or a fair, or a gallery space often located in a lush, green environment, like the Serpentine Pavilion in London's Kensington Gardens. Inspired by this transition from domestic structure to public building, the design for the first 'residential pavilions' in Formello expressed the twofold nature of the suburban home as a private dwelling and the place where collective individuality comes to be formed.Looking at the history of architecture, such a physical as well as conceptual separation between ontology and representation, intimate and civic dimension of the house recurs cyclically. If Mannerism emphasized this dualism creating a lucid deception, as in Palazzo Te and Villa Giulia's multiple facades, Postmodernism enhanced this separation fostering metaphorical syntaxes, as in Vanna Venturi House. Today an analogous crisis lets the fracture between real and virtual emerge, still unsolved. The utopia of global connection throws the private sphere into the public one, even if architects still hesitate to design this new paradigm, in other words the real-virtual space.

In the past years, I expressed the aforementioned dualism between intimate and civic dimension of the house through the elements of the shell and the porch, through a second skin that becomes the representation of the house, its media image. By adding a shell or a porch, the residence status loses its domestic dimension, analogously to the Palladian villas in Veneto, where the *portico* was co-opted from sacred or civic buildings and lent to the private house. In light of this, the shell can be seen as a cloak that shields the house from the

Lina Malfona, *L'architettura mancata*, 2011.

theme of the envelope. It has been defined as a 'residential pavilion,' a construction for residential purposes but also equipped with devices that transfer the collective dimension within the private one. The house therefore expresses the ideal of living together individually and becomes the place where collective individuality—or, to use Nancy's words, the «singular plural being»—comes to be formed.[16] If the fullness of the public sphere directly depends on the freedom of the private one, the suburban villa creates an eminently collective model, or better, a civic one.

After a first wave of people coming to the Roman countryside from Rome, we witnessed the relocation of more families moving to the Roman countryside from abroad. Families from Iraq, Holland and Sweden became MPA's new clients, while other families purchased some of the houses designed for the former clients, sometimes asking my office to make changes. The second phase of our work overlapped with a gentrification process and shows a progression in the relationship between typology and topology, between artisan practices and necessary standardization, between local cultures and global expression. These houses simultaneously reveal the author's need to take roots—which comes from the analysis of the Italian rural and vernacular tradition—and her immanent will to go across, in order to take a critical position on this tradition, this history, these places. Memories can help to make new histories, projected towards the future and capable of being local and universal at the same time.

According to Arjun Appadurai, the anthropologist who demystified the notion of modernization as a unique projection of the European and North American experience, the world map is redefined from time to time by the emergence of local cultures that were almost unknown in the past. We are witnessing that, instead of disappearing swallowed up by globalization, these local cultures are laying the foundations for building new cultural industries and new fields of artistic creation.[17] However, as I already said, recent postcolonial theories, which promote the study of these phenomena, have spread an overly orthodox attention on local dimension and identity. Today architects who work on a local area are no longer sedentarily rooted in that specific place. On the contrary, these authors move away from it, as I myself did, due to their need to create detachment, to look at that place with greater objectivity. In a way, even

16. Earlier in 1989, even Marc Augé wrote that a dwelling is above all a form of cohabitation. Cf. Marc Augé, *Ville e tenute, Etnologia della casa in campagna*, Milano: Elèuthera 2011 (I ed. *Domaines et Châteaux*, Paris: Éditions du Seuil, 1989), 109.

17. Cf Arjun Appadurai, *Modernity at Large. Cultural Dimensions of Globalization*, Minneapolis: University of Minnesota Press, 1996, chapter: "Here and Now".

18. Cf Kenneth Frampton, *Six Points for an Architecture of Resistance*, in Hal Foster (ed.), *The Anti-Aesthetic. Essays on Post-modern Culture*, Port Townsend: Bay Press, 1983.

19. Cf Fredric Jameson, *The Seeds of Time*, New York: Columbia University Press 1994, 202-203.

20. Please consider that this book frames a period earlier than the onset of COVID-19. At the moment we can only put forward some pale assumptions about what will happen to the physical and geopolitical map of the world, to the economy and to the debate on globalization.

21. Cf Georg Simmel, *The Stranger*, in id., *Soziologie: Untersuchungen über die Formen der Verge-sellschaftung*, Leipzig: Duncker & Humblot, 1908; Georg Simmel, *The Sociological Significance of the 'Stranger'*, R. E. Park & E. W. Burgess (eds.), *Introduction to the Science of Sociology*, Chicago: University of Chicago Press, 1921, 322-327.

local architects can be considered as relatively foreigners. In 1994, Fredric Jameson wrote a critique about Kenneth Frampton's distinguished theory on 'critical regionalism',[18] acutely arguing that this is a geopolitical proposal, since it works to mobilize a pluralism of regional styles, aiming at resisting standardization of what will be called 'late capitalism' or global corporativism.[19] If the first part of this statement can still be acceptable, the second part must be updated because today even the local dimension can assume a rhetorical or vernacular tone, becoming an instrument of capitalism. Even local architects can rewrite their history and 'use' their culture as a means of propaganda.

If it is true that globalization contributed to the final convergence of demand, it is also true that it has been the main engine in the discovery and spread of local cultures, totally ignored in the past. If we can argue that globalization has made the world homogeneous, it must also be said that today each point located on the global map has the same possibilities. If on the one hand globalization has a standardizing effect by supporting corporate organizations, on the other it promotes coexistence and syncretism, supporting the discovery of unexpected connections between distant cultures and heterogeneous areas. It would seem that continuous mobility has crushed the world map towards the center, bringing all places closer together.[20] If so, nobody today should feel or should be considered as a foreigner, a stranger. According to the philosopher Georg Simmel, the 'stranger' is the sociological form of the coexistence of mobility and fixity, proximity and distance.[21] But if in 1900 this was a marginal condition, today the foreigner describes a shared condition, that these projects try to interpret as one of the components of belonging. Nonetheless, people who have lived in small towns like Formello for many generations still see the new inhabitants who live on the hills outside of the center as foreigners, outsiders, (resident) aliens; those strangers live in different houses from theirs and dissimilar from that context, therefore odd, monstrous houses. However, this alleged otherness, which has been opposed and even denounced from the beginnings, has recently somehow been accepted. Just think that some villagers, living in this town for generations, became MPA new clients. This last achievement is undoubtedly significant for us as it shows that these architectures have been recognized, for better or for worse, as part of this landscape.

5. villa(ge) and archipelago

The suburban villa is the most complex form of individual living but also the one that typically is less regulated. Between nature and artifice, this single-family house mirrors the geography of suburbs: open to the landscape on the one hand, protected and self-sufficient like an island on the other. If the archipelago is an expression of reciprocal relations, the villa, like the island, reveals a search for autonomy. In fact, the main feature of an island is the boundaries that surround it, which can be irregular or regular, natural or man-made. In all cases, boundaries are not only physical lines of demarcation—as the hedge which marks the property and protects from intrusions and prying eyes—but also existential acts and, at the same time, cultural and legal actions that give a precise status to the portion of space enclosed. To this extent, consider those social and political practices which stood behind the sacred *limes* (boundary) of ancient cities. The term 'villa' shows a close affinity with the term village. The village is the most primitive form of collective living, the primary social unit, based on neighborhood relationships. These relationships are authentic although conflicting, as they are based on the possession of conterminous properties to be defended and controlled.

If the village feeds on neighborhood relationships, the archipelago is the form of isolated living. The archipelago adds a landscape attribute to the concept of living and defines an insular mode of settlement. Both the village and the archipelago are spatial archetypes and settlement models but, while the village is a choral space, the archipelago is made up of islands, which by nature are finite entities, with a semi-autonomous organization. Neighborhood relationships, which are imposed by logistical reasons, describe the 'closed' nature of the village, while the archipelago is qualified by an 'open' urban form, which can be found in isolated but connected housing models, in dialogue with the landscape. If the village's inhabitants risk getting trapped in the meanders of its streets—as in the narrow alleys of the Italian villages—the inhabitants of the archipelago are free to choose who to share their interests with, and especially whether to do so in a real or virtual dimension. However, since digital technologies have transformed the world through the introduction of 'virtual communities' and 'social networks', the village has gradually become a metaphor for the world, at least since Marshall McLuhan introduced the slogan 'global village'. But not even this expression

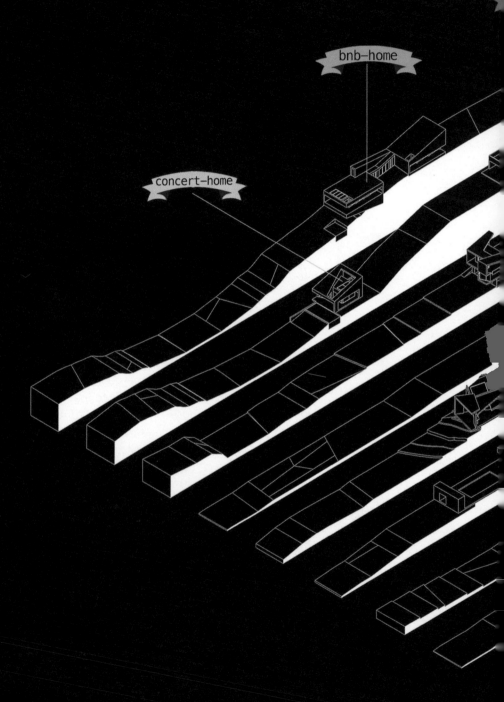

concert–home

bnb–home

Lina Malfona, *Village*, 2018

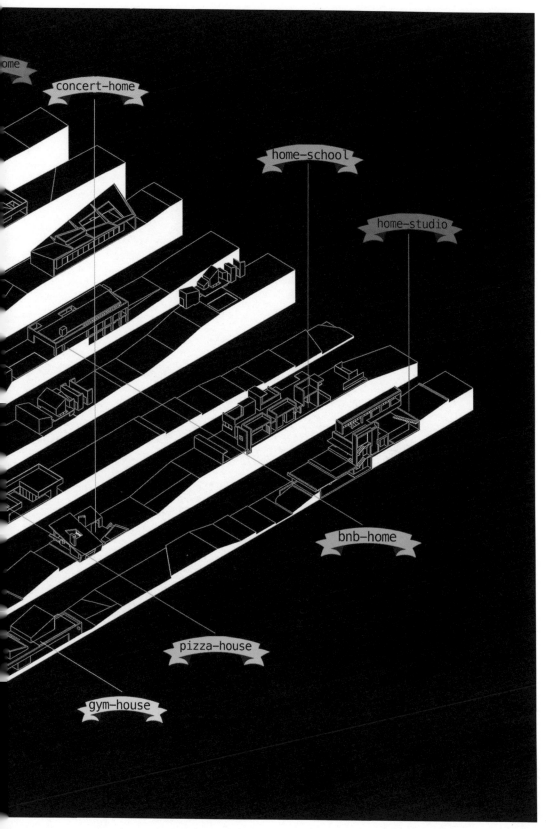

ome

concert-home

home-school

home-studio

bnb-home

pizza-house

gym-house

MPA, *The Aqueduct*, 2018.

Frank Lloyd Wright, Midway Barn in the Taliesin property, Spring Green, Wisconsin.

was used to underline the idyll of a finally reunited community but to highlight inequalities, disagreements and conflicts that the global village would have promoted.

Our speed-up today is not a slow explosion outward from center to margins but an instant implosion and an interfusion of space and functions. Our specialist and fragmented civilization of center-margin structure is suddenly experiencing an instantaneous reassembling of all its mechanized bits into an organic whole. This is the new world of the global village.[1]

Deploying the figure of the archipelago to explain the specificity of every single family house (*insula*) that MPA built in the small town in the north of Rome, I can show the process which led to the creation of a community intended as a collection of pieces. Each of the villas that make up this suburban constellation, surrounded by a large green area, is inserted in a low-density fabric. These autonomous and self-sufficient slivers create a sort of 'collage-city' which emphasizes the absence of territorial planning. Intercalated in this fragmented and dispersed territory—divided by narrow, labyrinthine and often unpaved streets, that reveal the spontaneous nature of the building fabric—these new 'islands' are instead rigorously designed and propose an alternative settlement strategy. As every island, every built property becomes a «pockets of optimal climatic and ecological conditions that allowed their inhabitants enough comfort to co-exist.»[2] In the previous chapter of this book, I formulated an idea of home intended as a relational place where 'collective individuality' comes to be formed, where the user can live alone and protected but at the same time feel part of a community. Linking together architectural typology and settlement syntax, even this archipelago, like every house it includes, can be read as a broad machine for living together individually.

1. Marshall McLuhan, *Understanding Media: The Extensions of Man*, New York: McGraw-Hill, 1964, 107.

2. Pier Vittorio Aureli, Maria Shéhérazade Giudici, "Island: The Settlement from Property to Care," *Log*, no. 47, Fall 2019, 175-199, 179.

3. The archipelago-city [città arcipelago] has been theorized by the Italian philosopher Massimo Cacciari. Cf Massimo Cacciari, *L'arcipelago*. Milano: Adelphi 1997. The archipelago was also used by the historian Vieri Quilici as a feature to read the city of Rome. Cf. Vieri Quilici, *Roma capitale senza centro*, Roma: Officina Edizioni, 2007.

4. Cf Walter Benjamin, *Unpacking My Library: A Talk about Book Collecting*, Hannah Arendt (ed.), *Illuminations*, New York: Schocken Books, 1969, 60.

5. The Agency for the colonization of the territory of Maremma Tosco-Laziale [Ente per la Colonizzazione della Maremma Tosco-Laziale] was created in February 1951. The area of Maremma extendsover a territorial surface of 995.390 hectares, from Lazio to Tuscany, including municipalities in the province of Grosseto, Rome, Viterbo, Pisa, Livorno and Siena.

Since any archipelago is characterized by absence of center,[3] it also describes a democratic and anti-colonial paradigm, which can be used as a strategy for densifying, mending and agglutinating the sprawling suburbs. If an archipelago can be seen as a 'system of solitudes'—as Nietzsche wrote about the Venice islands—it can also be explained as a collection, a 'magic encyclopedia'[4] which continually regenerates itself through the transformation of its components and the experimentation of new design typologies. The term 'collection' introduces an attribute of value, which is not related to the piece selection but directly to its design process. The act of planting trees and designing buildings is similar to the act of creating a collection. And analogously to the collector and the curator's eye, the architect's hand needs to be read only in filigree. Over time, the concept of form has indeed been absorbed by the concept of formation, which explains how this archipelago has grown over time in symbiosis with the landscape. The concept of formation allows us to understand the creative and construction processes as subjected to continuous variations and evolutions. These houses are formations rather than completed forms, generators of space rather than containers. They are samples of a design practice that uses architecture to stimulate new settlement matrices and new forms of life. Formation is an inclusive condition.

In recent years the suburbs—which span from rural villages to suburban settlements and archipelagoes—welcomed new forms of social engagement. In order to investigate these relations, it has been necessary to study physical artifacts, experiences, immaterial practices, and rituals which supported the rise of these new trends. It should be noted that the entire territory on which the archipelago of villas is located was originally agricultural land, parceled out and assigned by the Agency for the Colonization of the Maremma [Ente per la Colonizzazione della Maremma Tosco-Laziale] to the land workers who submitted requests, as a consequence of the Agrarian Reform in 1950.[5] This reform had profoundly changed the national property structure, extinguishing large estates [latifondo] and initiating appoderation practices:

In these lands closed between the Capital and the provinces of Livorno and Pisa, between the Tyrrhenian Sea and the pre-Apennine spurs, along a territory of about one million hectares, the landscape had melancholic accents.

There were areas that were known only to planes, sheep, shepherds and the rare families who found work there as laborers and workers.

[In queste terre chiuse tra la Capitale e le province di Livorno e Pisa, tra il Tirreno e i contrafforti preappenni- nici, lungo una dimensione territoriale di circa un milione di ettari, il paesaggio aveva accenti melanconici. C'erano zone che le conoscevano soltanto gli aerei, le pecore, i pastori e le rare famiglie che vi trovavano lavoro come braccianti e salariati].[6]

6. Ente Maremma (ed.), "Un Giorno in Maremma," 1966. http:// www.arsial.it/arsial/wp-content/ uploads/page/La-riforma-agrar- ia-nella-maremma-tosco-la- ziale-cenni-storici-1.pdf

The epic construction of a series of rural buildings [poderi] began on the agricultural lots assigned by the Maremma Authority [Ente Maremma] with the migration of hundreds of workers coming to the capital city and its hinterland. But later on, these buildings came to be irregularly turned into residential buildings and legally remitted, following a long series of amnesties. Around 2000, rural land was converted into building land, so a ravenous race to build hundreds of isolated villas began, visibly altering the per- ception of the rural landscape, now largely lost. Today this territory appears as a disseminated and scattered resi- dential fabric, where local houses replicate as automatons certain traits of vernacular buildings. However, this is not an analytical rereading nor reinterpretation of vernacular architecture—from the rustic farmhouse to the shepherds' hut—but is rather imitation, quotation, re-enactment. And finally, these new buildings—born as illegal houses or origi- nated from speculative operations addressed by rapacious builders—have visibly altered the ancient landscape and the tradition of rural houses and *poderi*.

These new constructions have also trivialized some features of vernacular building through the use of dazzling iron gates with little columns at their sides (and lions on top of those columns, generally); wrought iron arches and grates, often with rounded ends at the bottom; strange chimney pots and Tortoise capitals; pastel-colored plasters and false ashlar. The torn picture of this suburban area is similar to the de- scription of Santa Clara Valley, the present Silicon Valley, carried out by Reyner Banham in the eighties. Banham depicted the Valley's buildings as paradigmatic examples of egocentrism and formal excess, designed in a kitschy architectural style. He expressed a sense of disenchant- ment as good architecture either disappears, readily replaced by kitsch, or survives only to be "reused," as in

Lina Malfona, *Roman Countryside*, 2013

7. Cf Reyner Banham, "The Greening of high tech in Silicon Valley," *Architecture*, no. 74, March 1985, 110-119.

8. Please consider the studies carried out by Robert Venturi and Denise Scott Brown (*Learning from Las Vegas*, Cambridge MA: MIT Press, 1972) and, more recently, by Michelangelo Sabatino (*Pride in Modesty. Modernist Architecture and the Vernacular Tradition in Italy*, Toronto: The University of Toronto Press, 2011) on the harmonization of the vulgar and the Vitruvian components in the Italian landscape.

9. Cf Rem Koolhaas, Bruce Mau, Hans Werlemann, *S, M, L, XL*, New York: The Monacelli Press 1995, paragraph: *The Generic City*", 1248-1264": Against the notion of "Generic City" consider: Franco Purini, *La misura italiana dell'architettura*, Roma-Bari: Laterza, 2008, 37.

the case of Campbell High School, a classic-style building that was converted into a shopping center.[7]

With a starkly different approach, the elementary school in Formello—designed by Sergio Lenci in the sixties as an avant-garde structure, built in reinforced concrete—is about to be demolished because it would be too expensive to recycle or consolidate it. Analogously, the home that the renowned engineer Sergio Musmeci built for himself on the Formello's hills—a villa with a semi-spherical observatory on top—is pretty unrenowned.

In order to carry out an updated, dynamic and transversal reading of this particular region of the Roman countryside, the spontaneous and largely unlawful past cannot be overlooked.[8] The territory of Formello is indeed characterized by two different stories: the first one is the story of the landscape's artificial construction, which occurred through a large infrastructure project started in the Etruscan Age; the second one is the story of the absence of planning. Thus, this landscape has been deeply marked by the action of man, crossed by deep ravines, wells and tunnels. Much of the underground territory of Formello, indeed, is crossed by Etruscan tunnels, a complex system for the drainage and collection of water, linked to a set of wells for water supply. The image of this eroded land has also been a design inspiration for us: burrowed through, vertically and horizontally; a land that is in large part made of tufa, and therefore spongy, malleable, full of water. But there is also, as we now know, a more recent history, characterized by a widespread construction that imposed itself as an overturning of the heroic landscape handed down from the past. This area is deeply marked, indeed, by the intervention of improvised builders and surveyors (the Italian *geometra*) without a specific culture, who produced a myriad of houses without architectural quality and transformed the outskirts of the city of Rome into a «generic city,» similar to that so well analytically described by Rem Koolhaas.

A generic city is devoid of specificities and hence it is a ubiquitous and anonymous city that might be found in peripheral conditions, in fringe locations, in the post-colonial city or in the speculative city, according to Koolhaas. It is ultimately the «apotheosis of multiple-choice concept», «an anthology of *all* options.»[9] We should consider some further passages of Rem Koolhaas' writing, *Junkspace*, in which the author depicts the contemporary city as the place in which architectural themes

MPA, Built work in Formello

1. Fossi Vecchi social housing
2. Small pavilion for exhibitions
3. *La Villa*
4. *Camino dei Cardellini*
5. *Case binate al Monte Lavatore*
6. *Blue House*
7. *The Aqueduct*
8. *Villa Rosa*
9. *Case alle Terre di Bettona*
10. *Finestre sul fiume*
11. *La casa sul bosco*
12. *Casa al Praticello (Slot-House)*

and figures are recycled: a territory dominated by a wild, fragmented and unruly aesthetic, the place of the exasperated, naked and insulated typology.

Through my experience as an author and builder, I challenged the vision of a city as a pile of by-products of consumption through the instruments of design. My efforts have been directed towards reversing Koolhaas' analysis, a pessimistic reading that offers no alternative to resignation.

I trust that good design practices—which merge the study of architectural typologies and settlement syntaxes with social commitment and technical innovation—can trigger good behaviors. I employed the metaphor of the collection as a settlement strategy to place value in the center and reject the so-called 'junkspace'. Therefore, together with my office, I attempted to design the city through a bottom-up approach, creating synergies between building ethics and local engagement. The construction of a residential archipelago in Formello has been carried out through an intense commitment in the field and with the belief that good architecture can induce appreciable models of sociability. On the one hand, our commitment has been lavished on the making of a negotiated code between architects, clients, collaborators and manufacturers, all of them involved in managing this eminently local practice. On the other hand, I introduced and applied the model of the collection, intended both as a settlement strategy and as a conceptual device to characterize this open and expanding archipelago, this sort of «city by parts».[10]

10. About the notion of 'city by parts', see: Aldo Rossi, *The Architecture of the City*, ibidem, 35, 54, 100, 112-13.

To summarize the properties of this theoretical as well as physical device:

– the collection dismisses the generic and speculative city model;

– the collection is the product of a process carried out by an author, who leaves only a glimpse of his role in the final product;

– the collection merges landscape with architecture, using the metaphor of the plant nursery—in place of *Junkspace*—as a design tool.

6. the houses collection

These houses' apparent lunar landing in the Roman countryside is a stress test of language, a form of negotiation between formal themes and forms of localization.

Michele Calzavara, "Lunar Landing in the Roman Countryside", *Abitare* no. 588, 2019, 60-69, 62

1. Hans Ulrich Obrist, *Ways of Curating*, London: Penguin Books 2014, 57.

If the isolated villa is usually seen as the epitome of the remote control center, the residential archipelago is based on the idea of isolated but supportive living. Designing and building an archipelago of homes has indeed something similar to the act of creating a collection, a collection of pieces, held together by a series of relationships, often set up by a collector. According to the curator Hans Ulrich Obrist,

a collection is a way to conceive the world: the relations and the principles that inform a collection comprise assumptions, juxtapositions, discoveries, attempts at possibilities and associations. Hence, one might state that collecting is a method to produce knowledge.[1]

If the act of collecting can be seen as a method to produce knowledge, can it be considered a project?

Collecting can be deployed both as an hermeneutic lens to critically read residential archipelagos and as a design strategy. This topic brings us back to the drawing *Ichnographia Campi Martii antiquae urbis* (1757) by Gian Battista Piranesi, which can be read as the expression of an urban strategy that emphasizes the typological delirium of isolated buildings and the celebration of the unique piece, the one coveted by every collector.

Collecting can be seen as a settlement strategy in reference to certain 'suburban encyclopedias' of buildings, such as Villa Adriana, the grand residential complex which the emperor Hadrian built for himself in Tivoli. Villa Adriana is both a collection of places and a metaphor for the village, a complex arrangement of pavilions, gardens, arcades and squares linked each other. This construction was built in conjunction with the fall of expansionist craving during Hadrian's relatively peaceful reign, nevertheless, the Villa reveals the persistence of colonial thinking. On closer inspection, the reproduction inside Hadrian's suburban complex of those masterpieces that the emperor saw in Greece and in the East colonies appears as the expression of the emperor's respect and admiration for a common past, but this position can even be interpreted as a bloated expression of domination. This complex stretched around some thematic areas, including the ruins of an ancient republican villa that the emperor restored to insert it in the new system, the two imperial

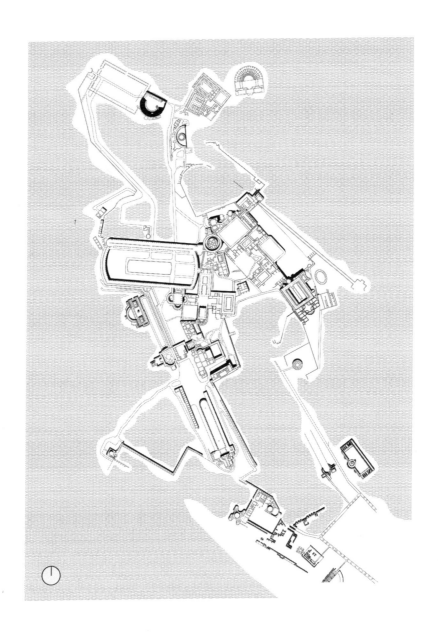

Villa Adriana, volumetric plan.

2. Cf Gregorio Froio, *La dimensione archeologica del progetto moderno*, Soveria Mannelli: Rubettino, 2013, chapter: "Villa Adriana e le ville della modernità," 167-280.

3. Cf John Jacobus, *Twentieth Century Architecture. The middle years: 1940-65*, London: Times and Hudson, 1966, 43.

4. Cf Bruno Zevi, *Il manifesto di Modena. Paesaggistica e grado zero della scrittura architettonica*, Venezia: Canal & Stamperia Editrice, 1998, 36-39.

5. Cf. Beata Di Gaddo, *L'architettura di Villa Borghese. Dal giardino privato al parco pubblico*, Quaderni di Groma, no. 5, Roma: Palombi, 1997.

6. Philip Johnson described his own work and declared his references in a 'visual' article published in *Architectural Review*. The article is from 1950, so it only focuses on the first two buildings, the Glass House and the Brick House. Cf Philip Johnson, "House at New Canaan," *Architectural Review* 108, no. 645, September 1950, 152-159.

areas, the Palace and the Academy, the Nymphaeum, the Golden Square, the Libraries and the Roman Baths among others. The composition of these residential areas—sometimes interconnected as parts of a village, sometimes juxtaposed as in a large collage—has become the inspiration for many architects, including Louis Kahn, Colin Rowe, James Stirling and Oswald Mathias Ungers, who have carefully studied the imperial villa as a collection of 'rooms'.[2] It is also interesting to mention Frank Lloyd Wright's transposition of Hadrian's complex in his project for Florida Southern College, as outlined by the historian John Jacobus.[3] It is a project that integrates geometry of architecture and geography of landscape, a useful project for Wright and an intermediate step on the way to envisioning Broadacre City. This further collection was the final expression of his thought on the relationship between city and countryside, urban planning and landscape design, typology and topology, of course an open project, perhaps a new beginning.[4]

One of the most interesting projects involving the use of collection as an architectural methodology is Villa Borghese in Rome, Cardinal Scipione Borghese's garden of delights. One of the largest public parks in the city, it can be seen as a collection of buildings—museums, fountains, small temples and pavilions, distributed along the key junctions of the roads—as well as a collection of diverse forms of green areas, from forests harbouring various plants to parks dedicated to peculiar animals (Park of the Fallow Deers) and large valleys (Valley of the Plane trees).[5]

Following a path traced by Villa Borghese and others public parks, many institutional and private park-museums are arranged around a series of pavilions located in large green spaces. Consider the Kröller-Müller Museum in Otterlo, designed by Henry van de Velde with its extensive sculpture garden and its scattered art and architecture pavilions, designed by Wim Quist, Gerrit Rietveld and Aldo Van Eyck. Consider also the Vitra Museum in Weil am Rhein with architecture pavilions of Frank O. Gehry, Tadao Ando and Zaha Hadid, among others.The same idea of creating a collection of masterpieces led the architect, curator and essayist Philip Johnson to conceive his Glass House in New Canaan as a collection of pavilions.[6] Although designed by Johnson himself, the Glass House's pavilions would appear as sketched out by different authors.

Villa Borghese, volumetric plan.

Johnson planned the whole Glass House as a sort of open-air Wunderkammer where visitors would be able to admire buildings that record different seasons of his production. Upon closer inspection, this appears to have been a programmatic choice, as if Johnson had deliberately decided to design a pavilion in the manner of Gehry, Gwathmey, or Albini, in order to build his own legacy in the form of a manifesto of his chameleonic and inventive personality. As in Hadrian's Villa, these objects seem to come from afar and appear as unique pieces, purchased at an auction by an expert collector.

A particular example of a city intended as a collection of peripheral micro-cities (satellite cities) is the one provided by Ebenezer Howard as a theoretical model for his garden city.[7] Self-sufficient villages and satellite cities are re-emerging even today as real possibilities, given the concomitance of economic crisis, pandemic events and the development of remote working. Thanks to the remarkable progress in the field of transport and communications, today it is easier, indeed, to reach certain peripheral areas, which in turn can be easily reached by public utility infrastructures (electricity, gas, fiber). In designing a "Group of Slumless Smokeless Cities" (1898), Howard formulated a radial diagram in which large highways led from the Central City to the centers of the garden cities, which were in turn connected by a ring-shaped road that linked them all. Farms, reservoirs, waterfalls but also psychiatric hospitals and health facilities, cemeteries, quarries and manufacturing areas were to be located along that road, immersed in a large belt presumably in the forest, so out of sight. If the concentric organization invested the entire layout of the planimetric scheme, it also defined the internal organization of the garden cities. Unlike the previous examples, this settlement is based on centralization as corollary to colonization, and the overall scheme outlines an alternative city, expanding over the countryside as a web, made up of different poles, each of which works as an introverted and exclusive machine. As a matter of fact, all the projects examined so far were conceived from the outset as contained or closed collections of masterpieces, designed by the hand of a single author.

But history teaches that the construction of residential programs can also be sponsored by a single patron or guided by a single director and designed by multiple authors.

7. The Garden City Movement spread in Britain since 1898, the year in which Ebenezer Howard published *To-morrow: a Peaceful Path to Real Reform*, reissued in 1902 as *Garden Cities of Tomorrow*. This movement promoted the building of a series of self-contained communities around the center of London and other cities.

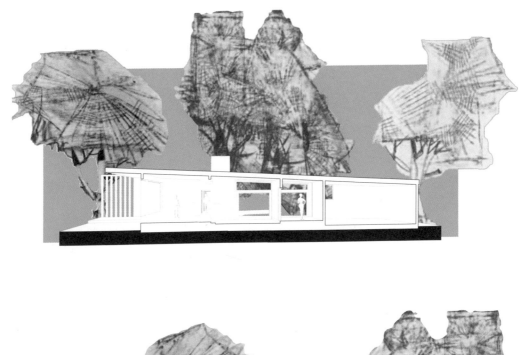

Richard Neutra, Case Study House #13: *Alpha House*, 1946.
Perspectival sections.

Consider the Weißenhofsiedlung, a model residential neighborhood built for the Deutscher Werkbund exhibition in Stuttgart (1927) and destined—as similar exhibitions—to last over time. Mies van der Rohe coordinated the whole design and construction and selected the architects involved in the project, which shows the relationship between architectural and social innovation promoted by the Modern Movement. Consider also the Case Study House program (1945-60), an experiment on the theme of the post-war house, which led to the construction of a number of villas, spread on a vast territory in Los Angeles.

In 1945, the director of the journal "Art & Architecture", John Entenza, understood that the period of reconstruction was the best time to inaugurate a renewal of architecture, so he launched the residential program "Case Study House Project" (CSH). The magazine directed by Entenza became the customer of this program which began with the identification of eight architecture studios, charged with designing the first houses of this program. The project attempts to put aside the artisan tradition and to use the most advanced technologies to create low-cost buildings for the American middle class. Two hectares of land were purchased to carry out this program, an area above the Santa Monica Canyon that faces the ocean. Architects and designers who joined the CSH program showed the effects of economy in design and proved that a good home can be made up of frugal materials, that outdoor spaces are part of architecture analogously to indoor spaces, and that a dining room may be less necessary than two bathrooms and large glass surfaces. All in all, the case study houses were small homes built with standardized elements. They were modular, linear, and stood out as distinct objects from the landscape, although California's lush vegetation soon took over.[8]

8. Cf Esther McCoy, *Case Study Houses 1945-1962*, Santa Monica CA: Hennessey + Ingalls, 1977 (1st ed. *Modern California Houses*, Reinhold Publishing Corporation, 1962).

More recently, the British initiative for the vacation homes program 'Living Architecture' has been involving many renowned architects in designing and building isolated villas in the countryside, as part of an expanding residential archipelago. In this last case there is a client, the philosopher Alain de Botton, whose aim is—similarly to John Entenza and Philip Johnson—to enhance the appreciation of contemporary architecture and to exploit the results giving people the chance to experience avant-garde architectures even for a weekend.

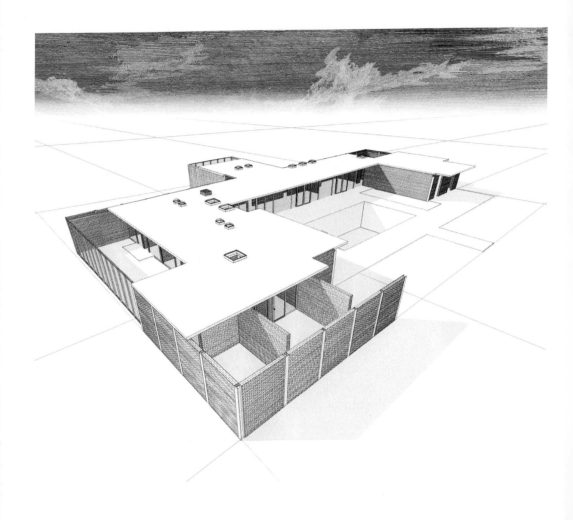

Craig Ellwood, Case Study House #17: *Hoffman House*, 1954-55.
Perspective.

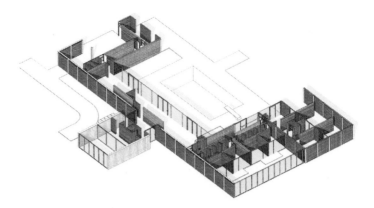

Axonometric View.

These three different patrons point out that collecting implies the presence of a collector who passionately studies, invests, catalogs and selects, with the ultimate goal of building her/his own museum. One might see a collection as the position statement through which a collector expresses his perception of the world, hence a collection finds its meaning in its subject.

In reference to the residential archipelago which lies in the Roman countryside, at the core of this book, one cannot fail to mention those collections of masterpieces gathered in the same geographical area, designed by a single author, and conceived as an evolving project. Consider the open residential archipelagos designed by Andrea Palladio in Veneto, Frank Lloyd Wright in Oak Park, Chicago, Mario Botta and Luigi Snozzi, both in Ticino. None of the these collections was conceived from the outset as a closed catalog, no overall planning decision was taken a priori and no masterplan was designed behind the overall enterprise. Generally these architects started their practice by designing their own home-studio or they responded to a client's request, and then they grew their network of clients and earn further assignments in the same area.

Each of the buildings belonging to these archipelagos has strong local roots. Its physical proximity is not accidental but it derives from the political action that architects exercised in that specific place, where they often played the role of negotiators, promoters, investors or entrepreneurs.

Consider, in particular, the complex human, work and sentimental relationship between Frank Lloyd Wright and his clients, reflected in the set of villas he built over time

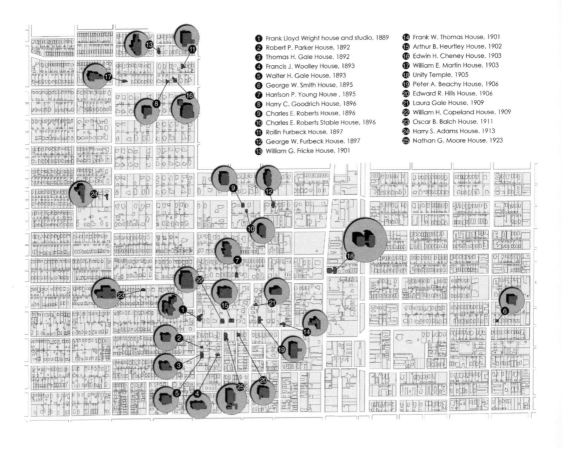

1. Frank Lloyd Wright house and studio, 1889
2. Robert P. Parker House, 1892
3. Thomas H. Gale House, 1892
4. Francis J. Woolley House, 1893
5. Walter H. Gale House, 1893
6. George W. Smith House, 1895
7. Harrison P. Young House , 1895
8. Harry C. Goodrich House, 1896
9. Charles E. Roberts House, 1896
10. Charles E. Roberts Stable House, 1896
11. Rollin Furbeck House, 1897
12. George W. Furbeck House, 1897
13. William G. Fricke House, 1901

14. Frank W. Thomas House, 1901
15. Arthur B. Heurtley House, 1902
16. Edwin H. Cheney House, 1903
17. William E. Martin House, 1903
18. Unity Temple, 1905
19. Peter A. Beachy House, 1906
20. Edward R. Hills House, 1906
21. Laura Gale House, 1909
22. William H. Copeland House, 1909
23. Oscar B. Balch House, 1911
24. Harry S. Adams House, 1913
25. Nathan G. Moore House, 1923

Frank Lloyd Wright, Villas in Oak Park, Chicago, volumetric plan.

in Oak Park, Chicago. The woman who later became his beloved partner, Mamah Cheney, was previously married to Edwin H. Cheney, who commissioned Wright to design the Cheney House in Oak Park. Among Wright's clients was the industrialist William H. Winslow, for whom he designed the Winslow House in Oak Park. Winslow was an inventor and he best embodied Wright's ideal of a self-taught technocrat. Another of Wright's inspirational clients was the real estate developer and construction contractor Edward Carson Weller, who principally sponsored Wright's early career. As Kenneth Frampton reported, in 1897 William H. Winslow and Waller together founded the Luxfer Prism Company, the manufacturers of the Luxfer Prism, which had a great influence on Frank Lloyd Wright, always interested in the use of large glass panels for both decorative and functional reasons. Winslow was also the creator of 'electroglazing', a system which reduces the refraction of glass, used in many progressive buildings, including Wright's Isidore Heller House. While managing the Winslow Brothers foundry between Oak Park and Chicago, Winslow was also a lawyer, amateur musician, photographer, and printer editor. In the basement of his house in Oak Park, Winslow started the Auvergne Press, which hand printed limited edition books, including an edition of *The House Beautiful* designed by Frank Lloyd Wright.[9]

9. This new edition framed the text authored by the distinguished Unitarian minister William C. Gannett with tapestry-like patterns designed by Wright. Cf Kenneth Frampton, *Modernizzazione e mediazione. Frank Lloyd Wright e l'impatto della tecnologia*, Terence Riley e Peter Reed (eds.), *Frank Lloyd Wright 1867 1959*, Milano: Electa 1994, 82-113.

10. Cf Leonard Eaton, *Two Chicago Architects and their Clients: Frank Lloyd Wright and Howard Van Doren Shaw*, Cambridge (Mass.): MIT Press, 1969, 39, 43-45.

Wright's clients were the expression of the non-conformist American middle class: sociable professionals, small entrepreneurs, inventors and industrialists. They were mostly 'action men', according to the Thorstein Veblen's thought, committed to produce things rather than accumulate power and culture.[10] Wright felt in tune with the urban-suburban way of living of these wealthy commuters, traveling between the congested traffic of Chicago and the bucolic quiet of Oak Park. Wright himself divided his time between office mornings in Chicago and afternoons in the quiet of Oak Park, where he could better focus on his own job, free from the distractions of the city. And very soon, actually, he left designing high office buildings to focus on suburban garden-cities.

Frank Lloyd Wright saw the single-family house as the expression of autonomy and individualism, but it did not have to express the clients' taste nor was it meant to be a mirror of their individuality. Indeed, the house had to reveal the architect's creative presence, and for this

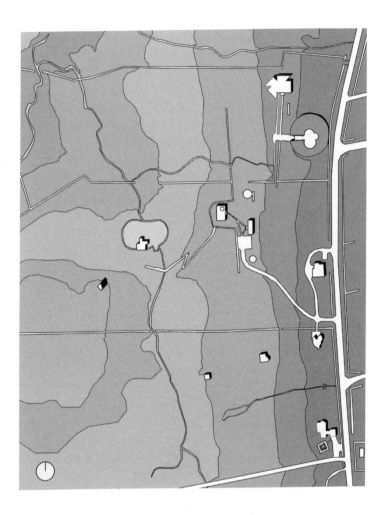

Philip Johnson, *Glass House*, volumetric plan.

11. Cf Gwendolyn Wright, *Frank Lloyd Wright e il paesaggio familiare*, in Terence Riley e Peter Reed (eds.), *Frank Lloyd Wright 1867 1959*, ibidem, 126.

reason the archipelago of villas for commuters built in Oak Park can be considered as an authorial repertoire of pieces of art, as a collection set up by only one author."
In the early 1900s, Oak Park could have been an ideal community or perhaps a garden city if in addition to the single-family villas Wright had been able to build collective facilities and public services, such as his Opera House, which was inaugurated in 1902 but which unfortunately was short-lived. Wright himself realized that to ensure civic dignity for such a community it was not enough to multiply single-family houses, so he designed a small dwelling that could be aggregated in groups of four residencies and that would be the primary cell of a larger fabric. This low-cost cell was published in "Ladies' Home Journal" in 1901, an event that gave wide visibility to his work. In Oak Park, Wright realized that a community cannot be characterized by a single social class and a single residential typology; for this reason, in addition to the detached houses, he designed a house that can be combined in series. In Broadacre City he took another step forward, alternating residential towers with single-family villas, also adding civic services, workplaces and farms to what became his blueprint for a model community.

The experience of Oak Park was extremely significant in the process of defining the single family house as a socially relevant, open, welcoming and sacred building. Following this experience, Wright developed a residential plan for a model suburb on the outskirts of Chicago, connected to the city via an electric tram. Unlike Oak Park, Wright formulated a plan for a city park, organized around the needs of a typical family and a typical neighborhood unit, an open plan welcoming immigrants who would have been compensated for the loss of their local roots.

When Wright finally left Oak Park for contingent reasons, ending up the first phase of his career, the architect decided to move with his partner Mamah Borthwick (Cheney) to Wisconsin, where he renovated his family estate in Spring Green, which he named Taliesin. From the concept of a community of houses Wright moved on to the idea of a home as a community, and Taliesin was the right place for building a Unitarian *coenobium*, according to Wright. Taliesin was a large complex made up of buildings with different programs that included a workshop, a school, a factory, a study,

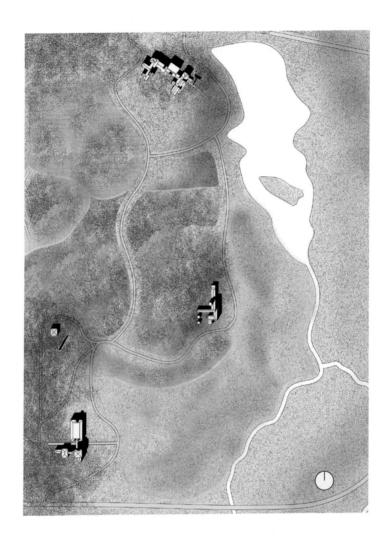

Frank Lloyd Wright, Taliesin East, Wisconsin,
volumetric plan.

Taliesin West, Arizona,
volumetric plan.

12. Kenneth Frampton, *Wright's Writings. Reflections on Culture and Politics 1894-1959*, New York: Columbia Books on Architecture and the City, 2017, 17.

13. Consider Giorgio Ciucci's criticism, taken up by Kenneth Frampton, among others. Cf Kenneth Frampton, *Modernizzazione e mediazione. Frank Lloyd Wright e l'impatto della tecnologia*, Terence Riley e Peter Reed (eds.), *Frank Lloyd Wright 1867 1959*, ibidem, 110. Cf Giorgio Ciucci, *The City in Agrarian Ideology and Frank Lloyd Wright: Origins and Development of Broadacres*, Giorgio Ciucci, Francesco Dal Co, Mario Manieri Elia, Manfredo Tafuri, *The American City: From the Civil War to the New Deal*, Cambridge (Mass.): MIT Press 1979.

a farm, a theatre, a residence. Like the Andy Wharol's Factory, Taliesin was a sort of 'production home', or better a place for living and working together.

From Oak Park to Taliesin in Wisconsin—and its winter analogue in Arizona—Wright's interest was always directed towards the ideal suburban enclave, based on private residence. And even in his latest rural utopia, Broadacre City, Wright envisioned the centrality of home and private property praying for one acre of land for every American citizen. Broadacre City was also a technological utopia, based on the use of automobiles to facilitate connections, telecommunications to avoid isolation and industrial production to supply consumer goods to mass customers. In fact, according to the words of Kenneth Frampton, Wright argued that «only an intelligent application of machine production would be able to redeem the excesses of mechanization, that is to say, would be able to imbue the mercantile nineteenth-century capital city with the essence of a soul».[12] In what was regarded as a regressive and timeless experiment,[13] and which instead was an extraordinary exhibitor of his most advanced ideas, Wright concentrated his vision on the dissolution of the boundaries between city and countryside. The most fascinating legacy of the pioneer who had the ability to build his own myth out of nowhere can be summarized in two points of his vision: the search for architectural quality in the suburbs and the idea of landscape as a collective issue. While his lifelong experience makes him the epitome of the 'creative engineer' who built one of the most fascinating images of the United States, these latter two aspects are what keep his lesson still alive.

7. private spaces for collective practices

1. Antoine Picon, *French Architects and Engineers in the Age of
Enlightenment*, Cambridge: Cambridge University Press, 1992, (I
ed.: *Architectes et ingénieurs au
siècle des lumières*, 1988), 278.

2. Antoine Picon wrote that
Ledoux's architecture "dominated the countryside, and
surveyed it, as was borne out by
the frequently repeated motif of
the belvedere, the observatory
or the mirador". Antoine Picon,
*French Architects and Engineers
in the Age of Enlightenment*,
ibidem, 274.

In 1804, Claude-Nicolas Ledoux published the first tome
of his treaty, *L'architecture considérée sous le rapport de
l'art, des moeurs et de la legislation*, where he inserted
his drawings for the ideal city of Chaux (1773-1806).
Around the Royal Saltworks of Chaux, the productive
complex built in 1778, Ledoux designed a network of
prototype residences and workshops located in the
forest. The aim of these "fabriques" was to reform the
habits of this region's "rude men," by promoting group
living and fostering corporatism. Ledoux designed each
home-workshop as a community place, around a main,
two-story-high space, with ovens for heating and cooking
at its center. As Antoine Picon noticed, «in the work of
Ledoux, architectural production began to be polarised
in terms of services and habitation, with the traditional
opposition between the monumental and the vernacular
being subsumed within the public/private dyad.»[1] These
houses' double program—the private and the collective
one—is strengthened by their visual permeability. In
Ledoux's house for the forest watchman—conceived
as an open cage where walls are replaced by pillars—
nothing obstructs the view of this rural panopticon.
In fact, the home-workshops' aim was to exploit the
productive countryside, and the forest in particular, as
a geography of energy sources. Thus, these houses can
be read contemporarily as private-collective places,
countryside control towers, and environmental sentinels.[2]

Around 1909, after the break with Oak Park, Wright
grasped that the privileged American middle class
was beginning to lose the possibility of building luxury
houses. Thus, the architect became interested in
technical reproducibility and modularity in industrial
production, processes that he could use to satisfy
the growing need for lower cost housing. Rather than
working exclusively on architectural form and landscape
integration, Wright began to focus on the economics
of form. But instead of working on rationalization
processes, based on industrial techniques, to be applied
to the entire building, he employed standardization
processes only to certain phases of the construction
process. Wright's idea was to provide the customer
with a solid, well-ventilated, and low-cost house, with all
the furnishings integrated into the architecture of the
building: in other words a turnkey house. Thus, starting
from the thirties, Wright experimented with a home

3. Cf Frank Lloyd Wright, "Usonian House for Herbert Jacobs," *Architectural Forum*, 68, no. 1, January 1938, 79.

4. Cf Carlo Carbone, "The Kit of Parts as Medium and Message for Developing Post-war Dwellings," *Histories of Post-War Architecture*, no. 4, 2019, 54-74.

5. Cf. Bill Olkowski, Helga Olkowski, and Sim Van der Ryn, *The Integral Urban House: Self-Reliant Living in the City*, San Francisco: Sierra Club Books, 1979.

6. Cf. Lydia Kallipoliti, *The Architecture of Closed Worlds, or, What is the Power of Shit?*, Zürich: Lars Müller Publishers and New York: Storefront Gallery for Art and Architecture, 2018.

for every USA citizen, the Usonian House, drawn in a manifesto published in *Architectural Forum* in 1938.[3] What differentiates most Prairie Houses—which marked the first phase of his work—from Usonian Houses is the architectural theme of the 'kit of parts.' This is a building technique as well as a design methodology based on the use of a set of elements, assembled following an additive process. Making buildings from a kit of parts would open the way to research on low-cost housing models that became a rule in the post-war United States.[4] But is the use of additive design processes—such as those based on a 'kit of parts'—the only way to lower the construction costs?

The Integral Urban House (IUH) was a pioneering architectural laboratory and a demonstration home, built following the post-industrial optimism for sustainable technologies. Founded in Berkeley in 1974, the IUH was an experiment in domestic autonomy, the attributive 'integral' standing for essential and self-sufficient. The building that would become the IUH was an old Victorian cottage that was converted into an urban homestead, equipped with ecological devices such as a composting toilet, solar-powered water heater, plumbing systems based on autonomous energy circulation, a bee hive, a freshwater pond, a chicken coop, a rabbit pen, and a vegetable garden in the backyard. Since the suburban single-family house has always been the American middle-class dream home, a symbol of prosperity and comfort, the architect Sim Van der Ryn together with an interdisciplinary team attempted to transplant the modes of suburban living into an urban context, and to inject ecological consciousness and energy efficiency into cities' domestic life. But the Integral Urban House was also a public showcase for systems and practices of urban self-reliance.[5] Rather than to privilege spatial design, the architectural elements, as well as the home occupants, were seen as potential energy transformers and the overall project was measured on the home's ability to operate as an closed ecological system.[6] Over time this "living laboratory" proved to be unsuccessful in practical terms as the activities that took place inside caused disturbance to the outside, making the house incompatible with the urban landscape. The legacy of this demonstration project was the spread of practices of urban agriculture and the consolidation of activist networks in the cities. However, the failure of IUH suggests that innovation does not derive solely from formal explorations, but nevertheless cannot ignore this aspect. Innovation comes from holistic integration and no architectural problem can be solved by hiding mechanisms for ecological sustainability within a nostalgic Victorian wrapper.

In the 1980s, the Californian writer, futurist and business-man Alvin Toffler formulated his utopian vision regarding the "third wave" of development for communication systems, which began with the advent of new forms of technologies that allowed spatial and temporal barriers to be overcome. Among other things, he proposed a new and systematic reflection on the home, understood as a place of residence, work, and entertainment at the same time. In a way anticipating the digital revolution and the effects of pandemic events, Toffler affirmed that new systems of production were beginning to take workers out of facto-ries and offices, putting them back in the home—or rather, toward what Toffler termed 'the electronic cottage,' a new idea of the home based on teleworking. His proposal would imply a complete transformation of all institutions, from family to school to the organization of labor:

The new production system could shift literally millions of jobs out of factories and offices into which the Second Wave swept them and right back where they came from originally: the home. If this were to happen, every institution we know, from the family to the school and the corporation would be transformed. [...] Yet this is precisely what the new mode of production makes possible: a return to cottage industry on a new, higher, electronic basis, and with it a new emphasis on the home as the center of the society.[7]

7. Alvin Toffler, *The Third Wave*, New York, Toronto, London, Sydney, Auckland: Bantham Books, 1980, 194.

This domestic utopia anticipated some of the most recent studies on the implications of labor, social practices and suburban settlements, and its relevance can be confirmed by the most recent achievements in smart working. But does this proposal help to soften the symbiosis between life and work in a countrified perspective or does it envi-sion a definitely dystopian perspective of a future with no more boundaries between life and work?

In January 2018, the Dutch architect Rem Koolhaas wrote the article "The future is in the countryside," published in a special issue of *The Economist*. In this text, Koolhaas denounced a lack of research on the countryside, which

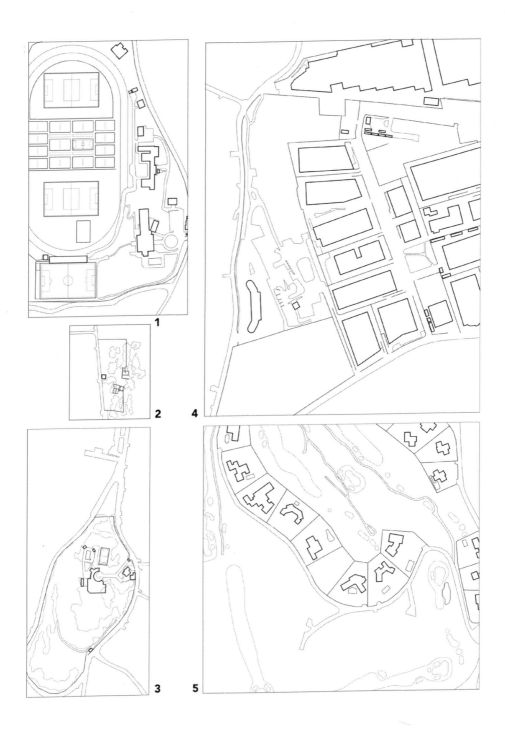

MPA, Yuzhen Zhang, Suburban analysis carried out on the territory of Formello.
1. Football Society "S.S. Lazio"; 2. Villa Chigi Versaglia (17th century); Villa of the former
Italian President Giovanni Leone; 4. Film studios and commercial district;
5. Olgiata Golf Club and residential area.

is changing much more radically than the city. According to his words, today's suburban space is the location for innovation, where the most radical transformations take place. Nowadays the countryside is the place where minimalist reorganization occurs and where we can see a proliferation of settlements that are growing with unstoppable Cartesian rigor. Thanks to new government policies, workers from other countries are re-populating these communities, revitalizing abandoned or previously uninhabited areas. All this results in a radical and all-encompassing transformation of suburban space, according to Koolhaas.[8]

In light of these four cornerstones of domestic innovation in the typological, economic, ecological and technological fields—read in the light of the Koolhaas' recent survey on countryside—it is possible to trace an alternative trajectory that climbs between the downtown congestion and the countryside isolation. Today the real challenge of design appears to be the creation of a peripheral architecture that reaffirms the value of the countryside within digital, technological society, so that living outside the center can become the premise for making new communities rather than mere *disurbanism*. Nowadays companies like Amazon deliver goods to one's house, and in the future technological development and widespread drone use will increase aerial transport, eliminating the need to live in the center in order to have necessary services nearby. Each suburban periphery will be central, as long as each house is supplied with a good internet connection and equipped with devices that allow drones to land and to be encapsulated within the dwelling-place, to flow products and goods. Soon then, every home would be disconnected from road networks—thus saving on infrastructures—since exchanges will take place through drones and aircrafts, which will probably become residences in a not-so-distant future.

Thanks to the development of technologies for long-distance transportation, many people will move from the congested city center to the countryside, where they can live in a peaceful environment, no longer undermined by the stress of the most urbanized environments, which however remain the physical center where cultural flows and creative collisions occur.[9] The ability to perform manual labor, such as taking care of green spaces and

8. Cf Rem Koolhaas, "The future is in the countryside," *The Economist*, January 2018, special issue: "The world in 2018," 153.

9. On the concept of 'collision density' see: Jane Jacobs, *The Economy of Cities*, New York: Random House, 1969; Richard Florida, *The Rise of the Creative Class: And How It's Transforming Work, Leisure, Community and Everyday Life*, New York: Basic Books, 2002.

making one's own house, might prove useful for increasing human beings' creativity but also to take a break from the grueling immaterial work. Similarly, workers' productivity might increase in the countryside, since everyone will develop interests outside of their field. Without neglecting context, local architecture culture and collective memories, the houses featured in this book consider the latest innovations in the field of unmanned aerial vehicles to implement an integrated design that incorporates technical thinking into design phylosophy, nevertheless a humanistic design.

In the latest work authored by Rem Koolhaas and his office OMA on this theme, the exhibition *Countryside, The Future*, the Dutch firm analyzes how cities will change when work as we know it disappears. This show took place at The Solomon R. Guggenheim Museum in New York, an exhibition space designed by the architect who has even managed to develop his own particular myth of rural utopia. The exhibition showed how cities, their topography, their demography and their collective rituals have been built around the idea of work as a concentration of human labor until today. But if physical work will definitely be replaced by automated work in the near future, then architectural typologies will have to change. Since human labor is going to disappear and digital communications infrastructures and online retail are taking over, many building typologies of late modernism—like factories, office parks and post offices—will soon look like ancient ruins to be eviscerated and allocated to different programs. When this will happen, co-housing and co-working activities will refill these buildings, according to the *Countryside* theorists.[10] Similarly, the country-house will have to be redesigned to host smart working, recreational and sports facilities.

10. Cf Niklas Maak, *Eurodrive: Repopulation Utopia*, AMO/Rem Koolhaas (eds.), *Countryside. A Report*, Koln: Taschen 2020, 56-61.

In light of these notable precedents, I am going to present in details the design and construction of a residential archipelago in Formello, a process that has been going on for more than ten years. It was determined both by local practices and universal design principles, which are independent from any place. Local practices mean commitment in consulting strategies, engagement in research in the field, support in processes of selection, purchase and sale of land, intermediation between owners of building lands in order to prepare wider construction programs. Over time, these actions have produced a connective tissue between architects, users, workers and local companies, activating a sort of permanent workshop, dealing with the development of this territory. But while this continuous workshop has made great efforts to create real conditions for building, the realization of collective interventions was limited to the building of a social housing complex and a small exhibition pavilion, both commissioned by an association of traders. Within the town center, many initiatives for setting up temporary stages for small summer events, public lighting and urban furniture have been launched, but unfortunately none of them has come to fruition. Outside the town center, collective spaces—such as a kindergarten, a football field stands, and a series of footbridges—have been carefully designed without ever seeing the light. History repeats itself and despite big efforts, initiatives in small towns are frequently thwarted. Even if the countryside is considered as one of the most privileged places to promote a communitarian approach, certain hamlets still work as exclusive places where you can build your own position only by belonging to that community, as in the most privileged club or in the most primitive clan.

When I moved to Formello, my experience in promoting opportunities of social engagement mainly focused on designing a new typology for the single-family house, conceived both as a formal construct and as a social product. The country house is a privileged place to find an almost perfect combination of autonomy, privacy, intimacy, green areas, landscape views, the presence of recreational activities and services. But today another program has taken on these features, the pervasive and all-encompassing dimension of work. According to Nicolas Bourriaud, today the spread of the home office is causing the artistic economy to undergo a reverse shift: the professional world is flowing into the domestic world, because the division between work and leisure constitutes an obstacle to the sort of employee that companies require, one who is flexible and reachable at any moment.[11]

If the small studio in the city is the main showcase of the creative worker, her/his isolated home in the countryside works as a productive zone: a garage, as in the best Californian tradition, a warehouse, an archive, a recording room, or a *hortus*. If in the past the suburban home was

11. Cf Nicolas Bourriaud, *Postproduction. Culture as Screenplay: How Art Reprograms the World*, New York: Lukas & Sternberg, 2002.

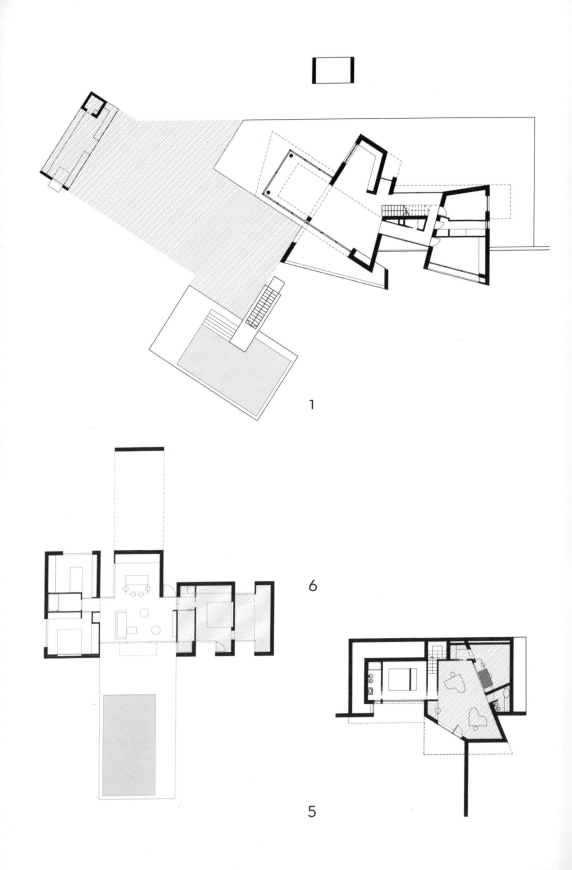

1

6

5

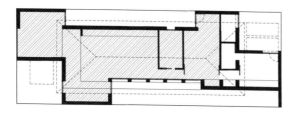

2

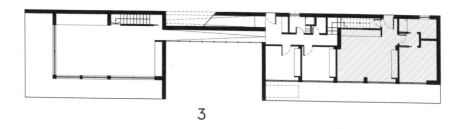

3

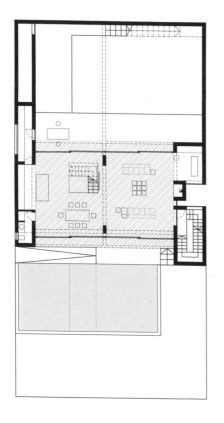

4

The *ultra-residential* dimension of the private house. The hatch shows the 'private/public areas'

1. *Villa Rosa*
2. *Casa al Praticello (Slot-House)*
3. *La casa sul bosco*
4. *La Villa*
5. *Finestre sul fiume*, Model B
6. *Case alle Terre di Bettona*

MPA, *Blue House*, living-working area.

12. On the concept of 'immaterial worker' see: Maurizio Lazzarato, *Immaterial Labor*, Paolo Virno, Michael Hardt (eds), *Radical thought in Italy: a potential politics*, Minneapolis: University of Minnesota Press, 1996, 132-141.

the place to cultivate leisure and hobbies, today the villa has become a production house [*casa di produzione*], the remote appendage of the urban outpost. Most of the customers of the houses designed and built in Formello are 'immaterial workers'[12], creatives and professionals who see their home as a place to feed the family, but also as a cave or a retreat in which to produce, store and above all work far away from distractions. As a slice of MPA commitment, the house designed for a singer (*Finestre sul fiume, Model B*, 2017) is divided into a public residence on the upper floor and a private workspace on the lower floor. The basement has been designed as a recording studio, a completely soundproofed, protected and poorly lit floor. «It is a sort of den», as the musician himself defines this retreat, where he can enjoy artistic privacy in a parallel condition to the total opening towards the landscape that he can experience in the upper floor.

In the architects' home-studio (*La Villa*, 2018), there are no boundaries between life and work. The house is intended as a total living-working area, a continuous environment in which all furnishing is designed as ambivalent device. Many workstations are distributed within the living area because each place can become the right one to capture creative inspiration. The entire villa is intended as a "production home" which houses a workshop-laboratory in the basement, a living area which doubles as a meeting room on the ground floor, a slightly independent studio on the first floor, used as a drawing room and recently as a smart working area.

La casa sul bosco (2018) contains a small apartment encapsulated within its perimeter, which is conceived as a 'small house within the house'. At present, this small multitasking annex is used as an independent home-studio for a family member, but this space may be used as a B&B or as a small exhibition area if necessary. The idea of endowing the home with a small self-sufficient space, contained in the very profile of the house—an object whose presence is imperceptible from the outside—has become a feature in designing suburban villas, a device that enriches the residential program with a public or collective complement.

But there is still another aspect to consider regarding the condition both individual and collective of our ultra-residential houses. The totally exceptional situation we are currently experiencing has made it necessary to transform the home—the background for distance lessons, interviews and conference calls—into a public place, with the consequent loss of domestic intimacy. This situation reminds us of the lost intimacy that Aldo Rossi noticed when looking at the buildings gutted by the bombing. The process that is making private life public is leading us to rethink our living space, from the physical space of the house, now invaded by cameras, to the virtual one where we can interact and meet people in full pandemic, a place that is still little explored and already overwhelmed by chichées. The pervasiveness of the virtual world, with online gyms and architectural backgrounds for video calls, will soon lead us to design a more defined and credible virtual space or, on the contrary, a completely surrealist virtuality, in which to test experimental solutions. Going back to the physical space of our home, to welcome prying eyes into the residence might reveal those essential fragments of our inwardness that instead we wish to protect. Thus, we might need to show only part of our space, cut it out, model it or stage it up according to the occasions. This transformation of the domestic world into a performative environment is already affecting our habits and our ways of living.[13] It is not only because of the risk of theft that all the houses that MPA has built in the Roman countryside are made up of a living room used as a work and leisure area—with large sliding windows and generally without a protected entrance — and a more intimate and reserved area, protected by an armored door.

13. Cf Luca Molinari, *Le case che saremo. Abitare dopo il lockdown*, Milano: Nottetempo, 2021.

The houses built in Formello have often been conceived as a dialogical system between a load-bearing core and an envelope, which is often designed as a strongly projecting structure, as in *La casa sul bosco* (2018), where the cantilevered area protrudes 9 meters. Generally these houses have a load-bearing structure in reinforced concrete with light infill, made of brick. Since it is a mixed structure, which cannot be left exposed, the house is generally plastered. This solution appears to be the one preferred by most clients, as it is the one that best balances the stringent needs dictated by the budget and the preference for a simple but expressive form. Attributes such as the nuances of handmade colors, their reflections under the light and the pastiness of plaster are still considered as features of high craftsmanship. Furthermore, the plaster technique makes it possible to perceive the house as a single body, a plastic object, a building made of a single material. *La Villa* is one of the few exceptions to this sort of rule. Here the mixed structure was, as usual, covered with plaster while the concrete structure was left exposed in the interiors. *Villa Rosa* and *La casa sul bosco* both show a aluminum skin, a solution that, on the one hand, increases construction costs while, on the other, eliminates maintenance operations, and which is therefore preferred by many customers.

All the construction processes are performed by local workers and implemented with local materials and techniques. This occurs both to provide the customers with an economic advantage and to promote local economies. Throughout more than ten years of work in Formello, MPA has been actively involved in implementing the local workers' knowledge through both educational workshops and active presence on the construction site. The result provided extensive benefits to many individuals: to workers, who have been enriched by the knowledge of specific and professional techniques; to customers, who have participated in the construction process understanding all its phases; to architects as well, who have learned more about traditional construction. The goal has always been the achievement of innovative, economic and long lasting construction techniques, which allow to save on construction times and labor costs without affecting the construction quality and the visual-tactile values, which are the artisan heart of MPA work. Also, this permanent workshop allowed young students to learn the construction techniques, from the initial design phases to the construction site.

An unusual feature of these houses is that, once the exterior painting is finished, and therefore the last can of paint has been used up, users have generally also exhausted their budget, which had been clearly rounded down. So even if the exteriors of these houses are completely finished—and equipped with all the accessories, including the lawn in rolls around the porch—the interiors are left unfinished and are often customized by the users themselves.[14] This practice recalls the way in which homes are built in the U.S., where they are designed as boxes with neutral and unadorned interiors because users wish to customize on their own. But here, in the Roman countryside, the double-sided effect is not a choice but rather a necessity that designers must

14. Customization is a post-production practice linked to the world of art and widely used as a design theme. Cf Nicolas Bourriaud, *Postproduction. Culture as Screenplay: How Art Reprograms the World*, ibidem, 39-45.

MPA, *La Villa*. Interiors.
Versatile furnitures.

consider from the beginning. On closer inspection, this practice can be read as the overturning of a consolidated building practice in Southern Italy, where people take the 'longest step of the leg' and begin to raise buildings intended to house two or three successive generations. The construction of these multi-storey houses inevitably stops after the construction of the ground floor due to exhaustion of the budget, once again underestimated. The result is yet another load-bearing skeleton, exemplified in the random constructions that punctuate Italian suburbs from Caserta to the south. These constructions leave the load-bearing concrete skeleton exposed and reaching up with its great gray bones. The consequence is the completion of the building's interiors only, when possible, while the exteriors remain unfinished, the reverse of what happens here, in the Roman countryside.

In addition to their private/public dimension, what makes these ultra-residential houses innovative is the synergistic relationship between architecture, engineering and digital technologies. This relationship determines the conditions for creating low-cost, energy-saving residences, almost completely disconnected from public networks, and therefore self-sufficient buildings. In many of these houses, passive systems, such as solar greenhouses and ventilation chimneys, have been used together with technological systems—underfloor heating, heat pumps, water recovery and purification plant, artesian wells, photovoltaic panels and solar thermal as energy supply—managed by home automation. Houses are detached from any type of network, except the electric one, just because experimentation in the field of energy accumulators fed by the photovoltaic system, which could replace the use of electricity, has not yet produced excellent results in terms of price performances. Of course, this degree of autonomy means that each villa can act as a self-sufficient island. One of the sharpest critics of American culture, Reyner Banham wrote the text *A Home is not a House* (1985), where he reported that thousands of Americans had shed the deadweight of domestic architecture and lived in mobile homes. The truly innovative compass of this phenomenon, according to Banham, is the disconnection of mobile homes from any network, which allows them to become an autonomous device as well as a stockroom:

If someone could devise a package that would effectively disconnect the mobile home from the dangling wires of the town electricity supply, the bottled gas containers insecurely perched on a packing case and the semi-unspeakable sanitary arrangements that stem from not being connected to the main sewer—than we should really see some changes.[15]

Thanks to the ultra-residential nature of each of the houses built in Formello—whose collective space contributes to the creation of a series of amenities in the suburbs—this archipelago could easily become an *offline village* in exceptional conditions. I believe that autonomy is the main feature of the project for a residential archipelago in the Roman countryside. But autonomy is not only linked to the creation of an independent house, detached from any supply networks. By autonomy I mean the responsible freedom of the author during the design process. I mostly achieved this degree of autonomy because of my heterogeneous design team, made up of professionals who acted synergistically as designers and general contractors, delivering—as Wright did with his *Usonian Houses*—a 'turnkey home' to the customer.

In 1888, Louis Henry Sullivan published a text entitled "Style" in the magazine *The Inland Architects & New Records*. Here the American architect defended the rights of his professional category by engaging in the formulation of a national code for the independence of the architects. In 1890, at the annual meeting of the National Association of Builders, Sullivan promoted a proposal that favored the stipulation of direct contracts between architects and specialist firms, in order to eliminate the intermediation of general contractors, who play a huge role in the planning, organization, and execution of the buildings. Sullivan stated his opposition to general contracting and subcontracting, and argued for independent contracting of «'master workmen,' 'mechanics,' 'craftsmen,' and 'artizans' [sic]».[16] In so doing, Sullivan disregarded typical business practices and embraced both collective efforts and organizations, taking Ruskinian ideology as a reference and a moral guide: *I say then, [...] let us not approve any system of contracting which [...] could tend to relegate that individual merit, that therefore triumphant energy of the artisan to obscurity. Let us not divert one ray of light [...] from the individual form of the master mechanic.*[17]

15. Reyner Banham, "A Home is not a House," *Art in America*, no. 53, 1965, 70-79, 75.

16. Louis Henry Sullivan, "Sub-contracting – Shall the National Association Recommend That Ita be Encouraged?," *The Inland Architect & News Record*, v. 15, no. 1, February 15th, 1890, 18-19.

17. Louis Henry Sullivan, "Sub-contracting – Shall the National Association Recommend That Ita be Encouraged?," ibidem, 18.

A lucid truth was hidden behind this distinctly moralistic proposal, a truth that Sullivan was among the first to perceive. If the architect assumes the role of general contractor—hiring construction companies and individual workers on his own—he will gain an increasing building quality and the overcoming of the cumbersome bureaucratic apparatus that encompasses the entire construction process as positive effects. I realized quite soon that if architects are in charge of the whole construction process—recovering this typically American practice—they gain the highest goals: the best workers are engaged, delivery times become shorter, the cost of the work thins and the quality of the building is directly controlled by the design office at all stages. On the one hand, this process entails an increase in responsibility for the architect—who must clearly know how to control all phases of the work—but on the other hand, it ensures the best result.

The construction of a residential archipelago in Formello represented the effort of a team of architects fleeing the city, looking for a segment of expressive freedom to convey their creativity, their autonomy and their beliefs outside of any apparatus. The principle of autonomy led them to introduce architectural quality in the outskirts of the city, to initiate renewal processes and to create a pioneering architecture of the countryside, which struggles to challenge «the subtle nonjudgmental conformism of ruling taste emanating from the center».[18] In this way, this group of architects, engineers, builders and craftmen hope to have given a profound impulse to the creation of a non-traditional community, a community of 'foreigners' who, while not sharing a collective memory, probably are likely to share a direction in which to go.

18. Kenneth Frampton, "Toward an agonistic architecture," *Domus*, no. 972, September 2013, 1-8; also published on *Domusweb*, October 3, 2013 (https://www.domusweb.it/en/opinion/2013/10/03/_towards_an_agonistic_architecture.html seen on May 2, 2020)

8. "Agonistic Architecture of the Periphery"

none of these houses
is as relevant as its
convergence to build a
community

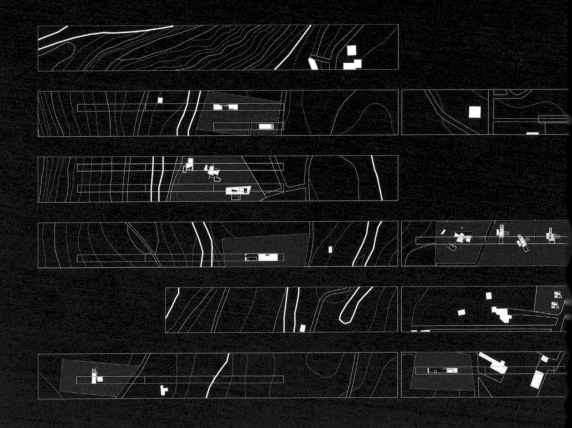

none of them
overshadows the
landscape and the beauty
of every olive tree

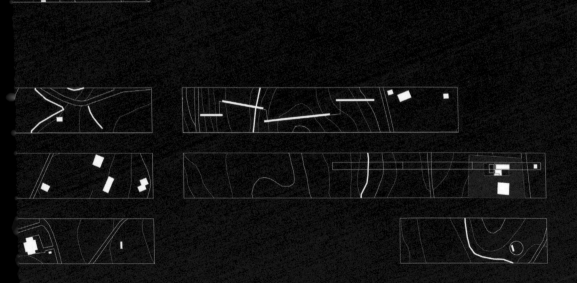

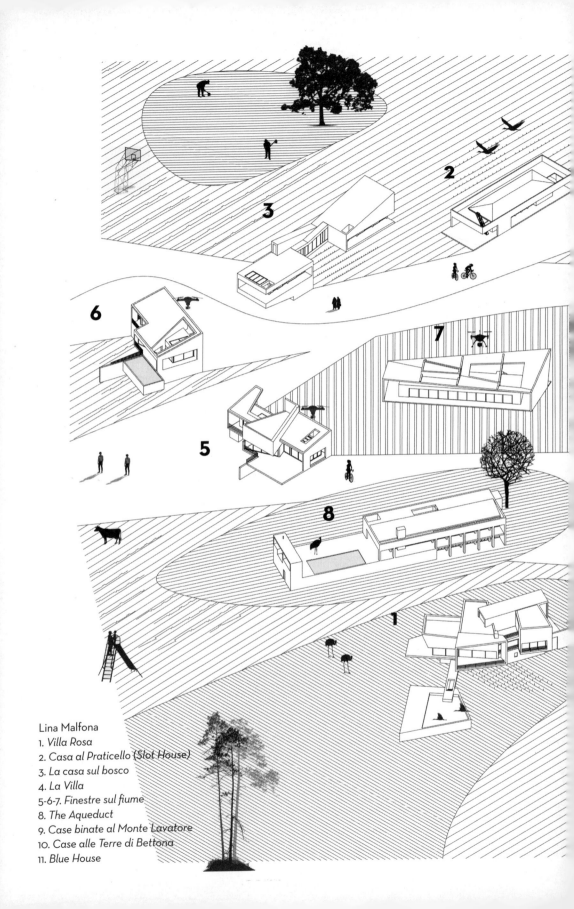

Lina Malfona
1. *Villa Rosa*
2. *Casa al Praticello (Slot House)*
3. *La casa sul bosco*
4. *La Villa*
5-6-7. *Finestre sul fiume*
8. *The Aqueduct*
9. *Case binate al Monte Lavatore*
10. *Case alle Terre di Bettona*
11. *Blue House*

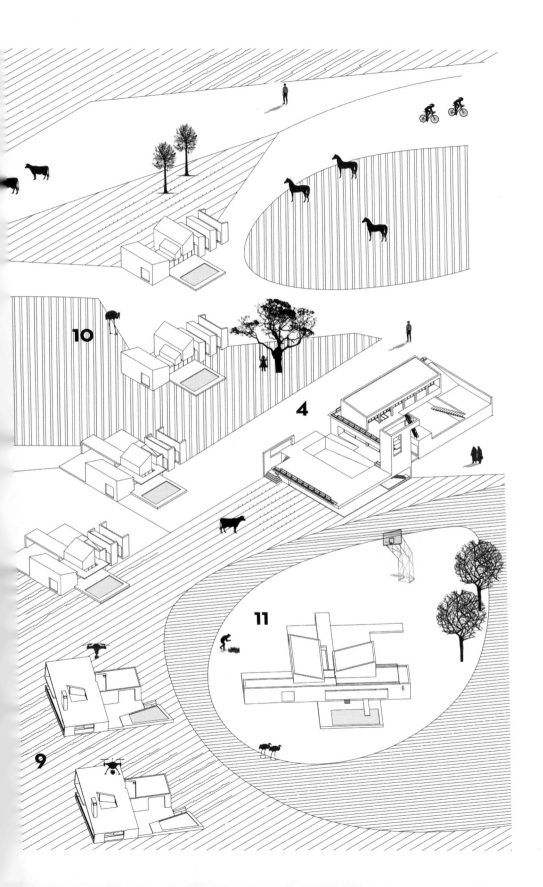

la casa sul bosco

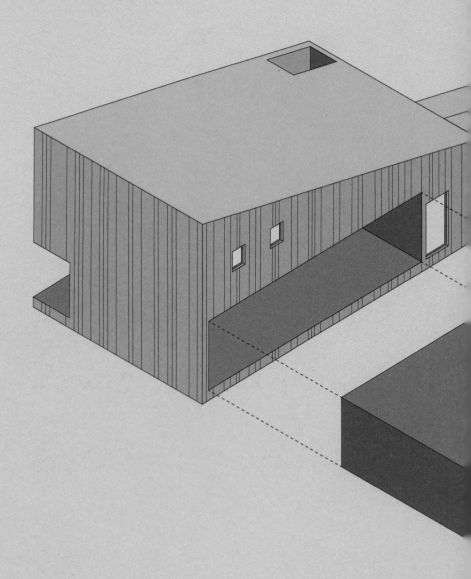

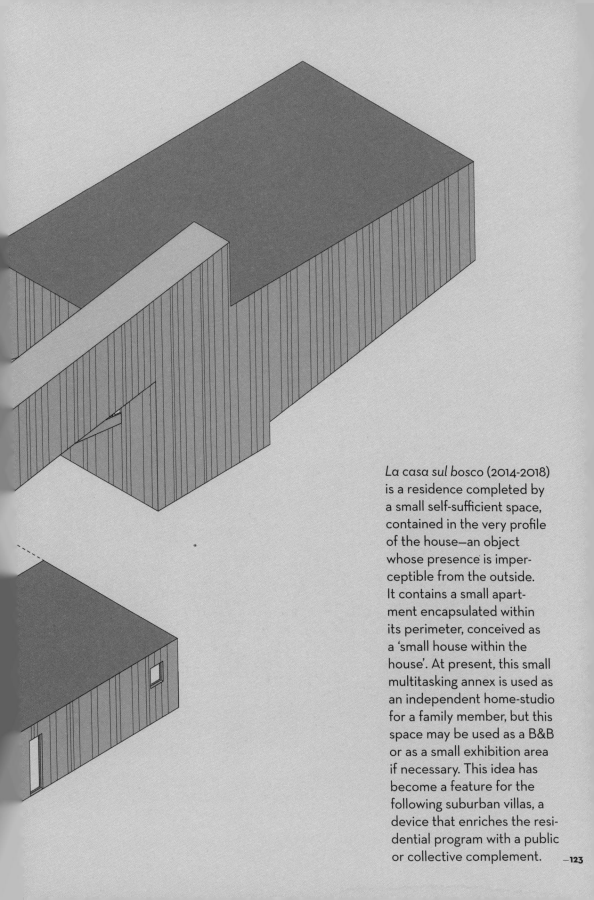

La casa sul bosco (2014-2018) is a residence completed by a small self-sufficient space, contained in the very profile of the house—an object whose presence is imperceptible from the outside. It contains a small apartment encapsulated within its perimeter, conceived as a 'small house within the house'. At present, this small multitasking annex is used as an independent home-studio for a family member, but this space may be used as a B&B or as a small exhibition area if necessary. This idea has become a feature for the following suburban villas, a device that enriches the residential program with a public or collective complement.

When the clients decided to move to Formello, they had not yet sold their house in the city. However, this young couple—an interior designer and a doctor— had long since drifted away from the city lifestyle, both for work reasons and for shared passions, including love for nature and care of green spaces. *La casa sul bosco* takes advantage of the unevenness of the land to get arranged on two volumes— the first one resting, the second one cantilivering—linked by two ramps, the first one connecting the sleeping area to the living room, the other one leading from the entrance to the roof terrace.

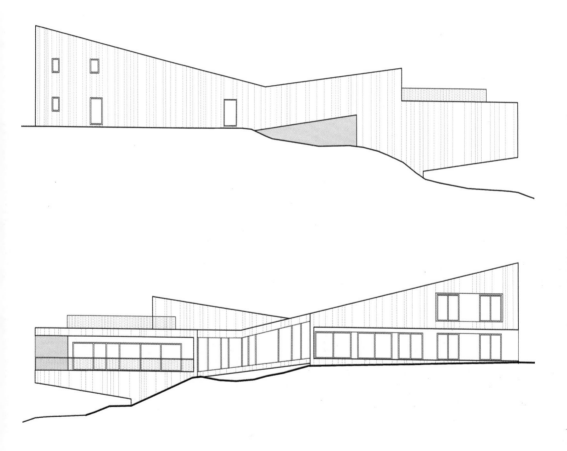

on the left
NW view.

on the right
N facade.
S facade.

on the next page
S view, detail.

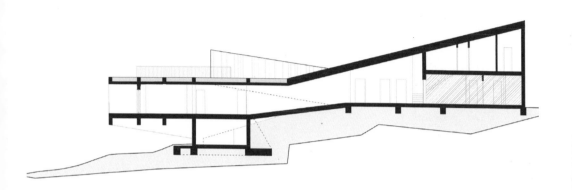

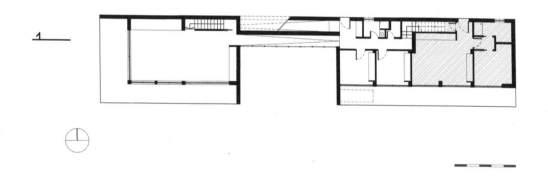

on *the left*
N view, detail of the living room's
hanging structure.

on *the right*
Longitudinal section.
Ground floor plan.
The hatch stands for 'private/
public areas'.

on *the next page*
view on the living area.

villa rosa

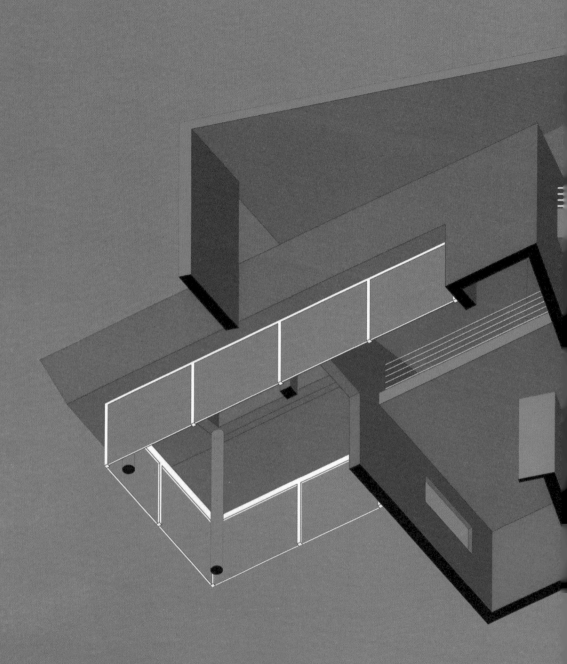

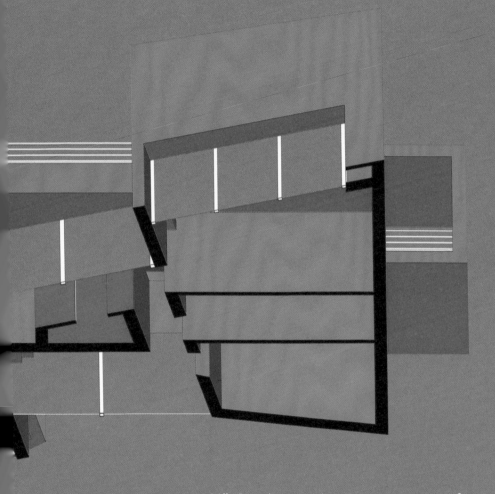

Villa Rosa (2012-2017) is an
architectural complex made
up of a series of pavilions
located at different altitudes,
inspired by the plan for Villa
Adriana in Tivoli. The main
pavilion, the residential
one, is supported by a large
basement—which is partially
underground—and in turn
divided into two different
areas, which are defined by
separate roofs, connected by
terraces and stairs, located
inside and outside the home.
The house's supporting structure is made of concrete,
and it is covered in white
plaster and aluminum siding.
Villa Rosa tries out a number
of devices that capture the
landscape, in order to frame
different sections of the
surrounding countryside.

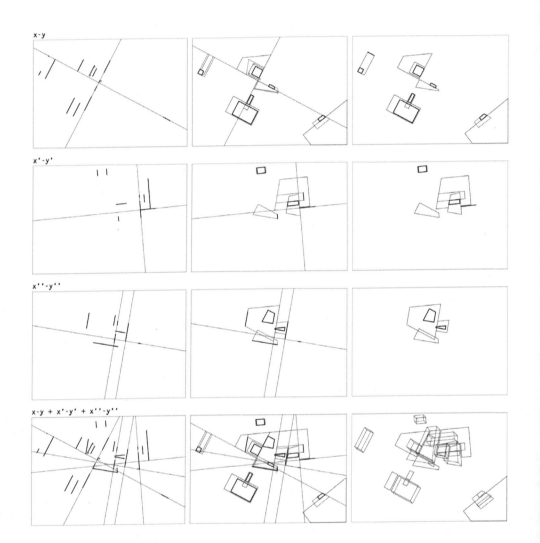

on the left
Lina Malfona, *Planimetric Tales*
(compositional diagrams), 2012.

on the right
SW view.

When Paolo and Cristina reached Formello, they intended to buy a large prefabricated wooden house. However, the high costs of this solution, on the one hand, and the advantages offered by a by a custom design, on the other, pushed them to go through the design process with our atelier. Over 7 years, this house has become not only an earthly paradise—with a green park with more than 300 plant species and a large vegetable garden—but also a creative factory, where users delight in building furniture for their own property in their free time. The home is spread over three levels and houses residential programs on the two upper floors while leaving complementary programs—such as the garage, the workshop and a small wellness area—in the basement. An outdoor kitchen completes the houses's complementary programs, rereading the ancient concept of adjacent areas, such as *pertinenze* and *dépendances*. This house is equipped with the most advanced technological devices in the field of bioclimatic architecture. The greenhouse, together with the underfloor heating, heat pumps, water recovery and purification plant, photovoltaic panels and solar thermal as energy supply, as well as any household appliances are managed by home automation.

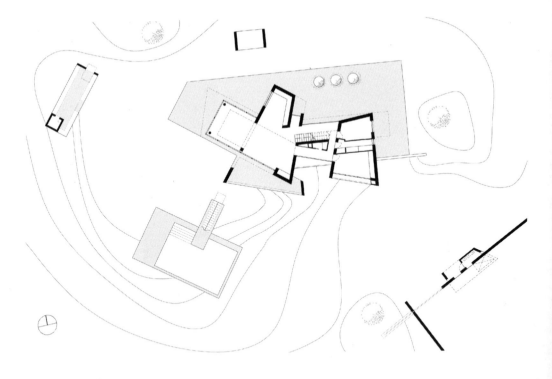

on the previous page
S view. Balcony detail.

on the left
General plan.

on the right
S detail of the terrace.

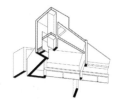

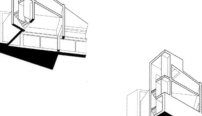

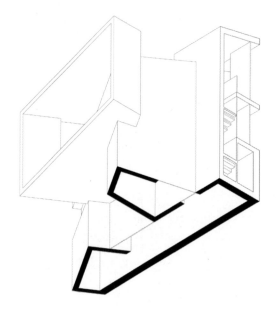

on the left
Axonometric tales.

on the right
Interiors. The living area.

on the next page
NE view toward the entrance.

blue house

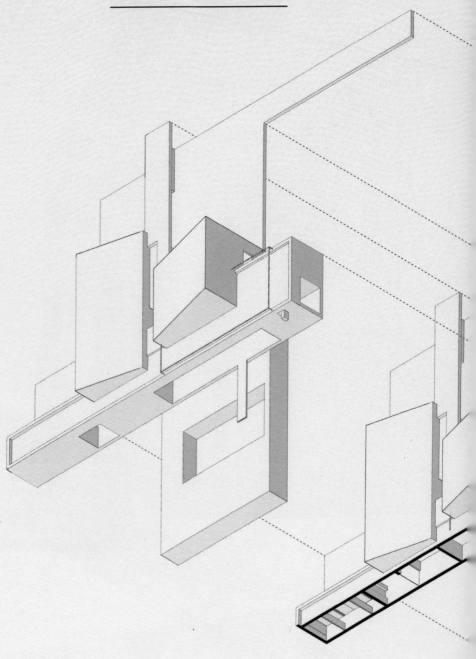

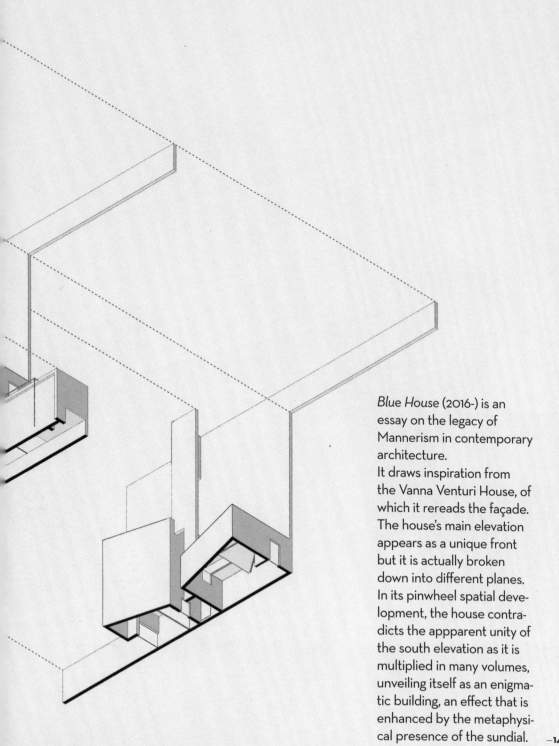

Blue House (2016-) is an essay on the legacy of Mannerism in contemporary architecture.
It draws inspiration from the Vanna Venturi House, of which it rereads the façade. The house's main elevation appears as a unique front but it is actually broken down into different planes. In its pinwheel spatial development, the house contradicts the appparent unity of the south elevation as it is multiplied in many volumes, unveiling itself as an enigmatic building, an effect that is enhanced by the metaphysical presence of the sundial.

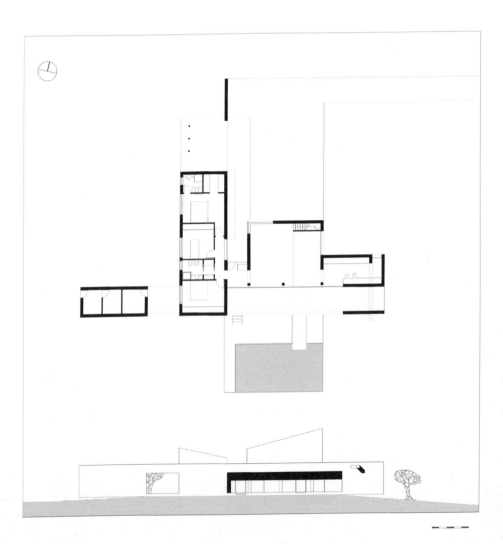

on the previous page
S View, detail.

on the left
Ground floor plan and S Elevation.

on the right
N View.

on the next page
E View.

case alle terre
di bettona

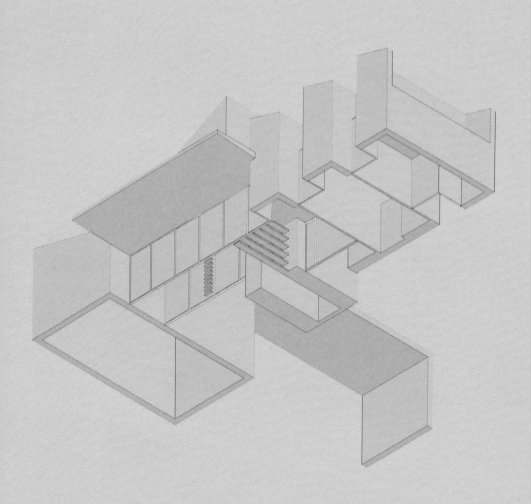

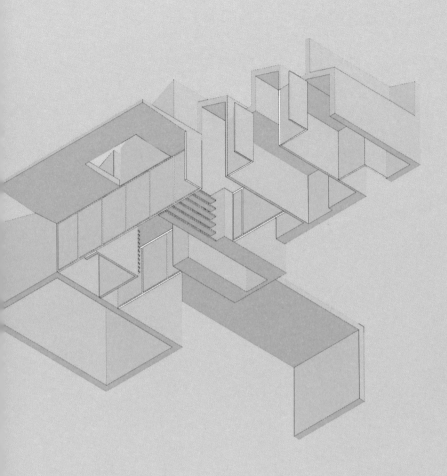

The client who commissioned the design of these houses (2015-) is a young couple of local builders who bought a piece of land to build a series of single-family houses along a hill. Having to design four houses placed one after the other, we imagined designing a continuous house, a sort of crenellated line which would then be sliced into four sections, obtained by bending the profile of the roofs. Each room in the house is defined by the sloping pitch of its own roof. The highest point of each house shows the position of the living room Each house has its own swimming pool and its external car port. Each of them has a mini apartment encapsulated within its perimeter, which can be rented as a b&b.

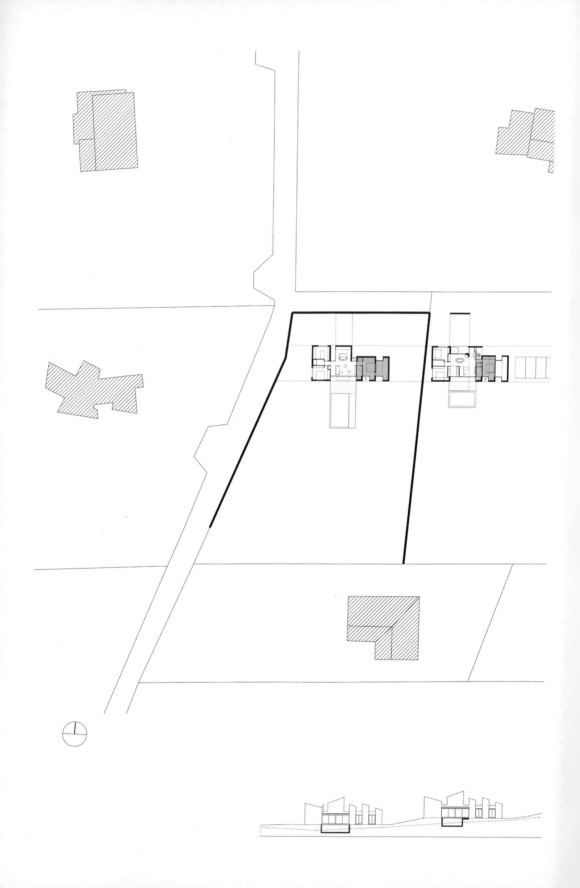

MPA, General plan of the
complex. The hatch shows the
'private/public areas'.

South profile.

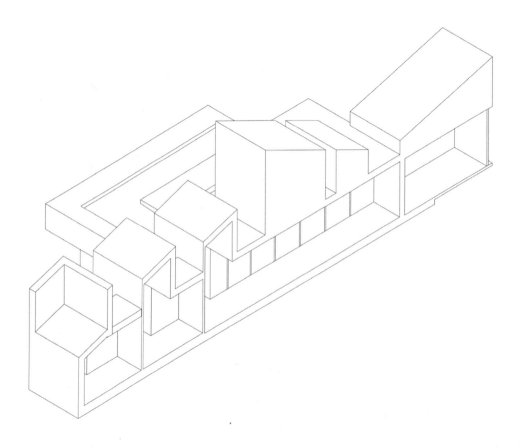

on the left
Axonometric view.

on the right
S View of one of the two built
houses.

on the next page
S-E View.

the aqueduct

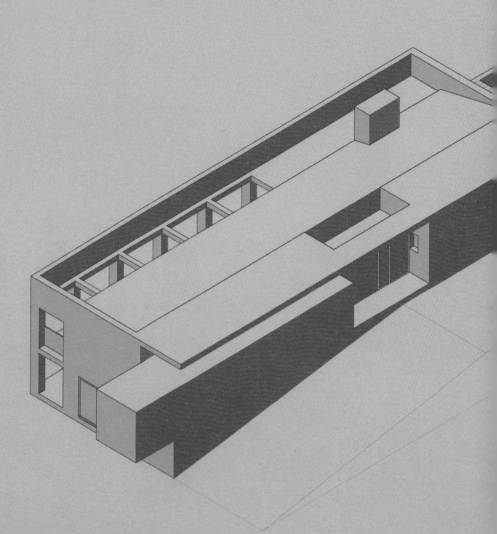

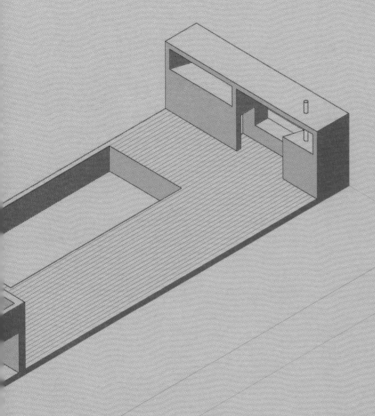

The *Aqueduct* (2016-2018) is a single-family house. Analogously to the *House for the Barrels Manufacturer* by Claude-Nicolas Ledoux, a house shaped as a barrel, this villa is designed for a builder of bridges and tunnels, and its long façade recalls the shape of certain territorial infrastructures. The client's job and his extraordinary stories of gigantic construction sites have undeniably influenced the design actions. The image of a piece of infrastructure slipping between the landscape's wrinkles—similar to the ruins of Roman aqueducts that line the countryside with their solid shadows —has long stimulated the architects' imagination.

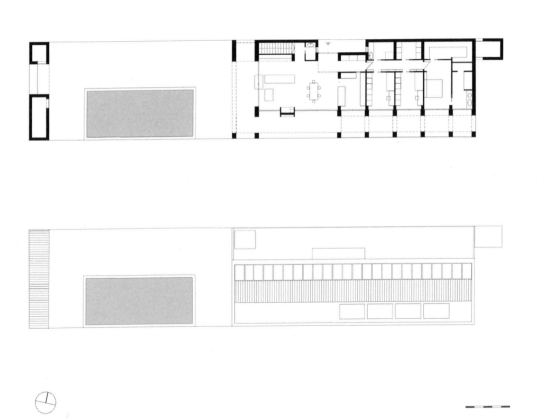

on the left
Ground floor plan.
Roof plan.

on the right
E view.

on the next page
SW axonometric view.

The project stages a dialogue between an elongated architecture and a landscape dominated by a deep valley. The house is designed according to the will to look at the valley, on the south side, and the need to be shielded from the winds, on the north side. The result is the creation of two different facades, which explore the conflict between heresy and dogma, rule and exception. The south façade shows a rhythmic system of pillars, which follows the rooms' large windows. On the north side, the house is almost completely closed and characterized by the excavation of the entrance, obtained by the translation of a volume, which cantilevers on the east side, like a sliding wall. The west elevation ends with a portico overlooking the swimming pool. This 'apparent' elevation is shielded by a second facade, belonging to a small pavilion which further extends the planimetric shape of the house beyond the swimming pool. This pavilion, used as both an outdoor kitchen and a dressing room, contains a covered and sheltered overlook, from which to contemplate the landscape. Its origins date back to certain suburban buildings, from shepherds' huts to the colorful facades of the Italian vernacular. But it also refers to the Giulio Romano's small *loggetta* in Villa Lante, Rome. Looking through this volume, one sometimes recognizes the white line of grazing flocks on the top of the hills. In the space that divides the infrastructure from the cottage runs the vertigo that links the territorial scale to domestic intimacy.

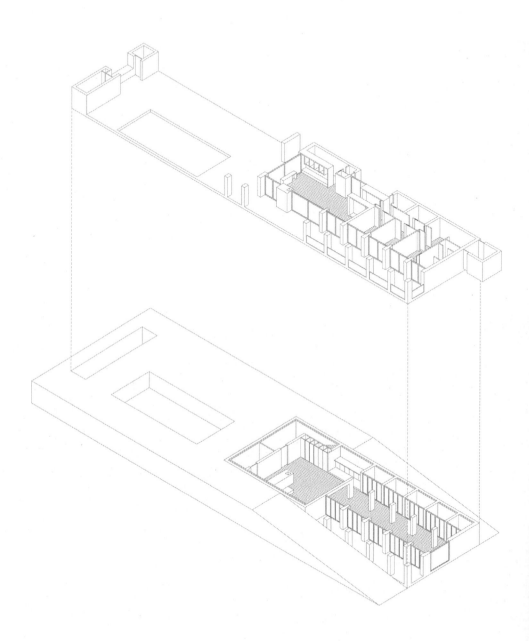

on the previous page
The small pavilion with its outlook.

on the left
Axonometric views of basement
and ground floor.

on the right
S view, country detail.

la villa

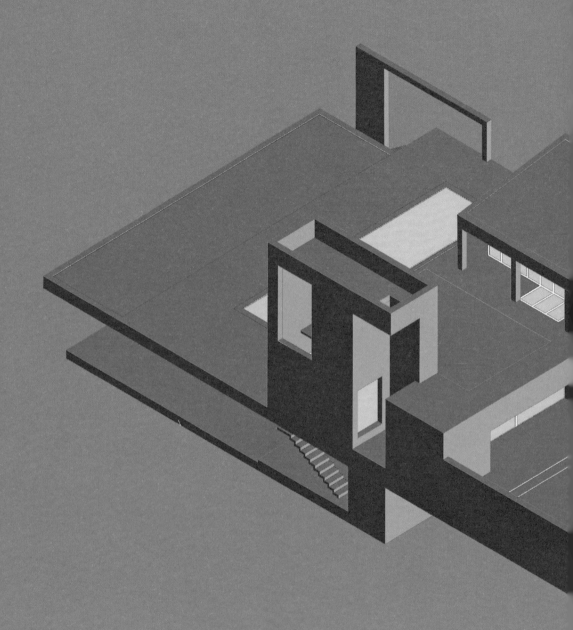

'La Villa' (2014-) is the name of the area where this home-studio is located. The house engages in dialogue with Villa Versaglia, one of the suburban villas belonging to the ancient Chigi family, situated on the opposite side of the street, Via della Villa. The 17th century villa is made up of a series of pavilions arranged around a wide open space, a courtyard. The main feature of this large complex is its entrance: the dovecote tower. Like the ancient Villa Versaglia, the new building develops around a patio and is dominated by the impressive presence of a tower, which connects three different levels. Initially conceived as a residence, during the pandemic this house has been turned into the architects' studio and research lab. Although it is already inhabited, *La Villa* is not yet completed and never it probably will as it has been designed as open and unfinished work.

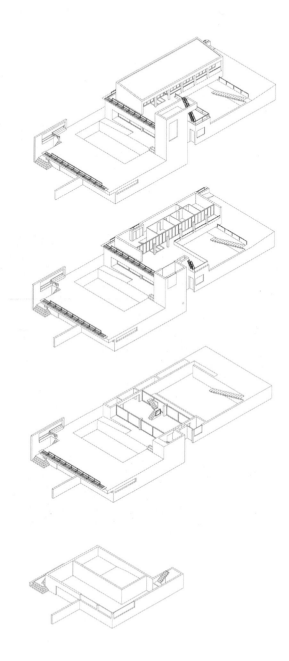

on the previous page
S view

on the left
Exploded axonometric view.

on the right
SW view with the ancient tower in
the background.

View from the patio toward
the living-studio

on the left
View of the living and working
area.

on the right
View on the stairs leading to the
drafting room.

la casa al praticello
(slot house)

La *casa al Praticello* (2012-2017) is a residential pavilion made up of a canopy, held up by pillars, and conceived as a large terrace. Beneath this terrace, the residential cells can be arranged according to the model of the Greek temple set up in a postmodern version, as an assembly kit of parts: the *crepidoma*, the *cella*, and the *peristasis* of columns are the elements. The house's nickname—*Slot House*—recalls the additive nature of this design: over time the house's components or rooms can be assembled beneath the canopy as in the motherboard of a computer. This canopy is intended to be both a tech-nological device and a way to access the house from the sky.

Slot House is a residence designed for a young tradesman with disabilities in locomotion. In order to optimize the use of space, this home has been designed as a compact object, arranged on a single floor. The house has two porches, one used as a covered carport, the other as an outdoor living room. The project recovers an existing vernacular building, which has been enveloped inside a new structure that still allows a glimpse of the old roof through the large openings made in the canopy.

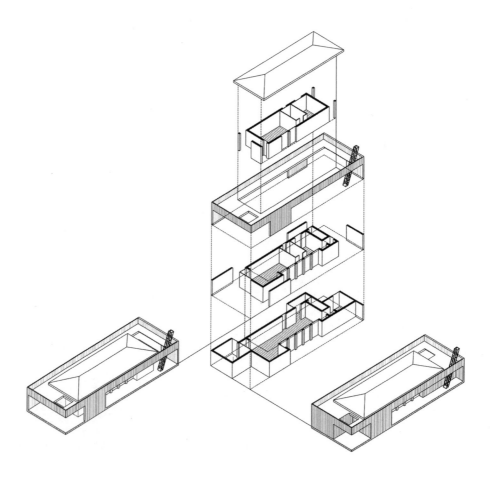

on the left
Exploded axonometric views.

on the right
W view.

on the next page
S-W view.

case binate
al monte lavatore
(twin houses)

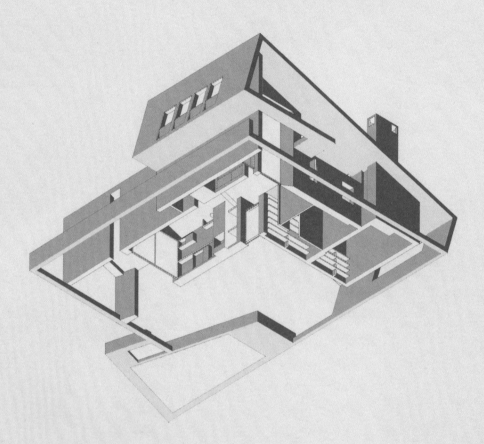

This design stages a sacred conversation between architecture and the landscape. Architecture wordlessly tells the story of the landscape surrounding it, through lines that trace borders and frame figures. Large openings pierce the twin houses, so that one can gaze out and frame shadows and horizons of the Roman countryside.

The *Twin Houses* (2009-2012) are three floors high, with an L-shaped floor plan that allows them to be expanded over time. In the violinist's house the exterior space is used as a stage for open-air concerts. The houses' peculiar roofs are covered in slabs of travertine. In the house for the fashion designer and her family, the two flues have been turned into ventilation chimneys.

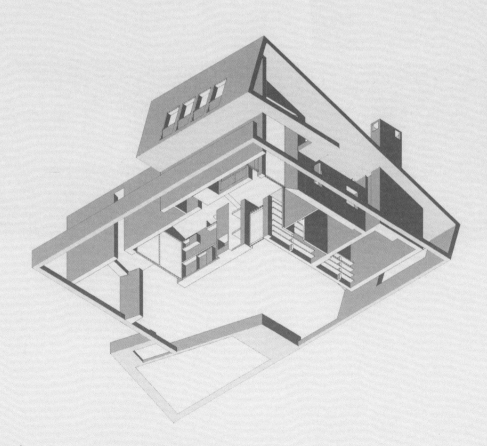

on the left
N view.

on the right
N-W view.

on the left
Plan cutting the first house's first
floor and the second house's
ground floor.

on the right
Exterior detail with the chimney.

on the next page
S-E view.

finestre sul fiume
model C

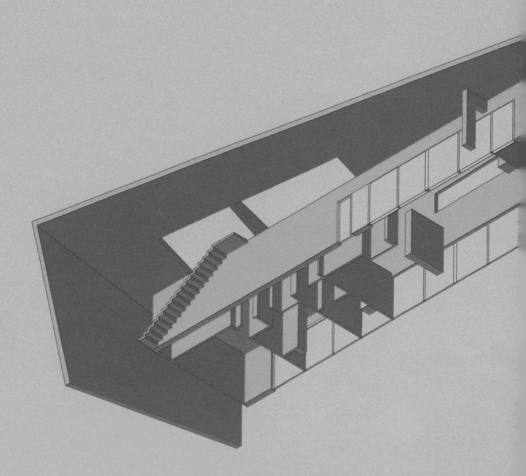

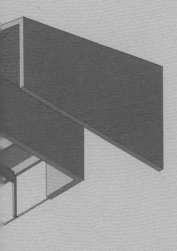

The residential complex *Finestre sul fiume* (2012-2017) is made up of three houses which play three variations on the same subject. They engage in conversation with living beings, drones, and a landscape molded by the ancient Etruscan engineers. The memory of Etruscan waterways is impressed on the houses' double roof, which is also a technological device allowing drones to access the house from the sky through home automation. It also blocks the wind and filters the light of the sun. Nevertheless, these three houses are oriented in a way so they can capture the highest quantity of light, as sunflowers. Each house has high energy performance (NZEB, nearly zero energy building) because they integrate architecture and engineering, thanks to the synergy of different techniques, including those related to the construction of the building envelope and the use of renewable sources. Thanks to the use of local materials, techniques and craftsmen, the houses can also be considered low cost and kilometer 0 homes.

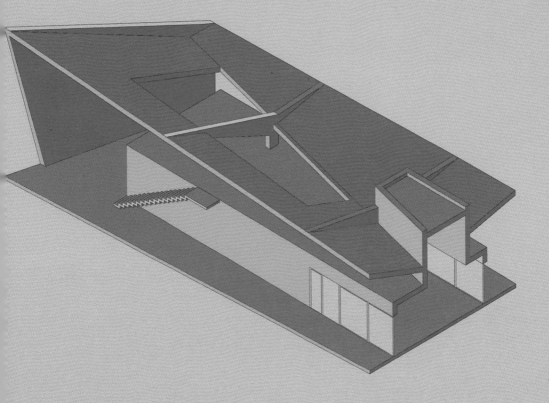

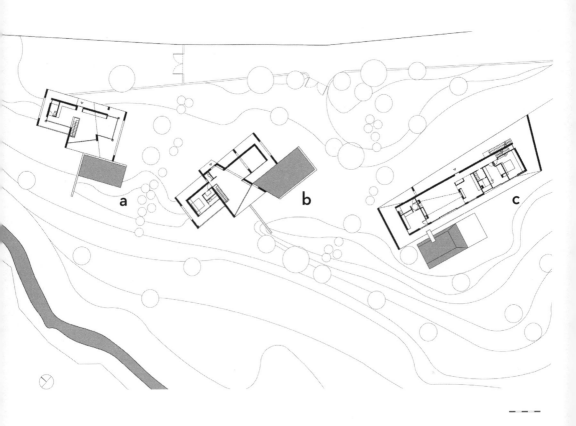

a

b

c

on the left
Ground floor plan.

on the right
View of the houses from the
opposite side of the river.

on the next page
House C, N view.

These three houses draw inspiration from open-air exhibition pavilions, little theaters and small buildings that can be found in parks, like those newsstands, kiosks, shrines, and aviaries that pop up in Rome's Villa Borghese, not very far from here.
The term 'pavilion' comes from the latin *papilio, onis*, which means butterfly.

The roof of each of these three houses recalls the form of a butterfly as well. This project rereads certain vernacular aspects of the Italian country houses—in particular the geometry of their roofs and the shape of their verandas—turning these ordinary aspects into an innovative, sensitive, and highly performative architecture vocabulary.

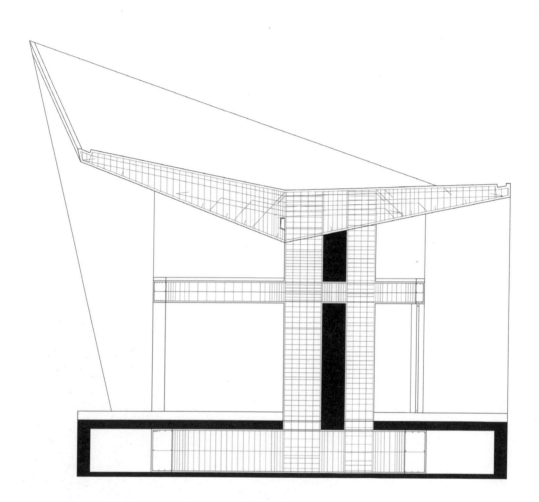

on the left
Tommaso Malfona, House C,
engineering cross section.

on the right
Lina Malfona, *Frame 02*, 2014.
First version of House C.

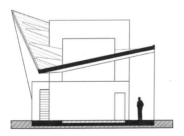

villa C

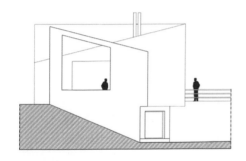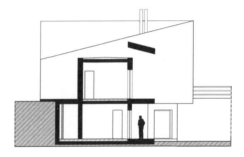

villa B

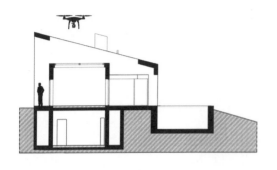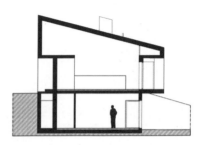

villa A

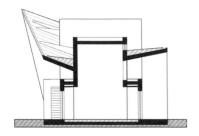

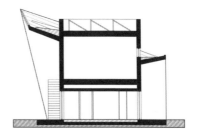

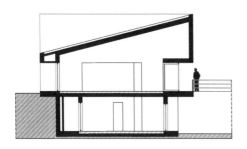

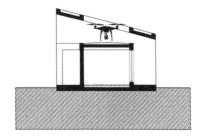

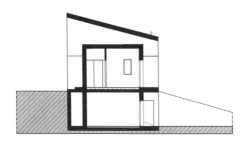

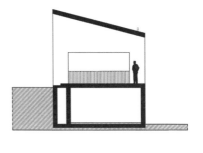

Lina Malfona, House A, B, C.
Taxonomy of cross sections.   —**211**

finestre sul fiume
models A-B

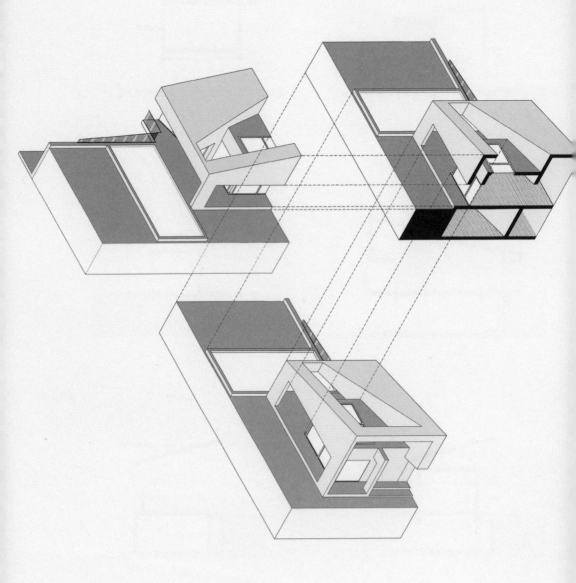

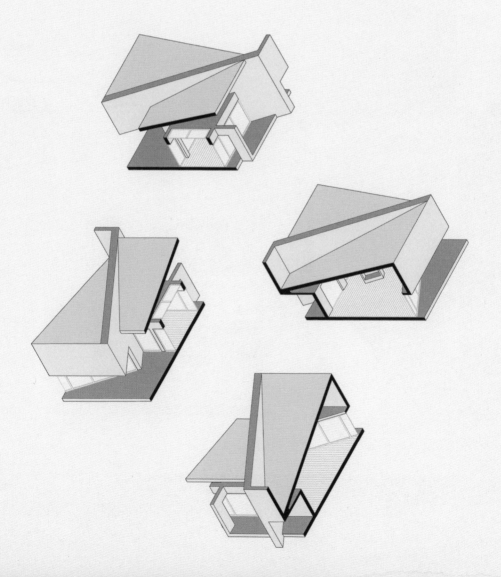

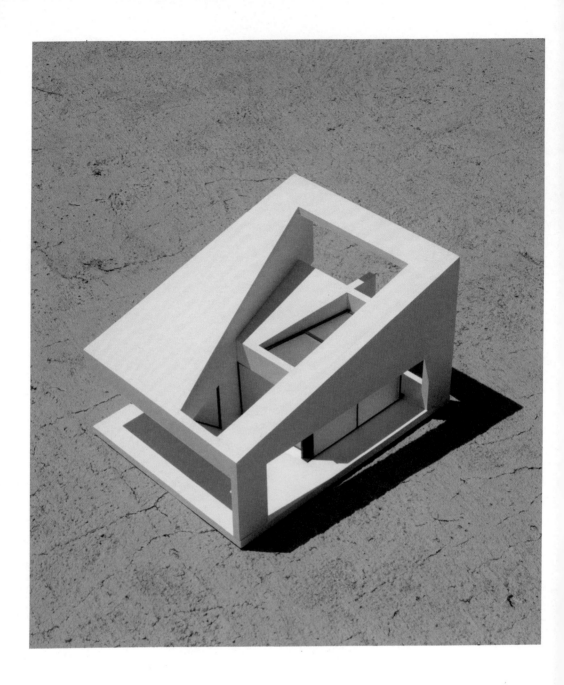

on the previous pages
House A, N elevation detail.
Etruscan waterwell in Formello.

on the left
House A, the porch, model.

on the right
House A, the porch.

on the left
House A, living room.

on the right
House B, living room.

on the next pages
View from House A to House B.

9. postscript on the end of the city

Lina Malfona, *Letter from the bushes*, Ithaca, Upstate New York, April 24, 2016.

Assuming that aerial transportation will replace road and rail flows, the villa must be both a dwelling and a station. Therefore, its roof should be designed as a device to access the house from the sky, equipped with a landing strip and large holes that allow drones to transport goods inside the home. The image of a roof intended as the fifth elevation of the house, which frames a sky that will soon be populated by drones and other gizmos to come, does not seem so far ahead. But this idea does not arise only from a particular attention to the integration between technological apparatus and typological-morphological layout, this futuristic imagery has its deep roots in the town of Formello's Etruscan past. The capable Etruscan builders continuously shaped this land: they sliced it in many directions so that they could move at different altitudes and from on high, they could descend through their *tagliate*—deep incisions in the ground—into the depths of the soil.

At the height of the advancement of studies and experiments on drones and unmanned aerial vehicles, urban growth will stop, cities will become immense ruins and roads will be transformed into green tongues. The image of the city will not be able to be anything other than the new version of Piranesi's Campus Martius, a territory without any urban trace.

The world's geography will gradually shift away from the congested center of the city. Architectural projections will be centered around the suburban villa. There will no longer be any train stations or airports but every house will also be a station. Because of this, the strengthening of the individual's residence will be the fulcrum of architectural experimentation and the house's cover, in particular, will be the very location of transformation. It will be the landing pad of individual transportation, and later the landing pad of the house itself.

Lina Malfona, 3 *Drone-Friendly Houses*.
Drawing for the Italian Pavilion, Venice Biennale, 2021

Residential cities will be demolished by walking factories—enormous neighborhood-grinding-machines that will carry out urban regeneration operations, moving from one place to another—and after that, they will become hills or artificial mountains.

The working city will be made up of groups of skyscrapers of hotel-offices, equipped with a number of facilities, cultural activities, and entertainment areas.

Outside of the city there will still be the possibility to acquire lands where one can erect new buildings, which will be thought of as future landing pads for drones. The countryside around the city will be punctuated by archipelagoes of residential pavilions, whose basic unit is a terrace from which to look out at the countryside.

At first, these terraces will function as covers to residential pavilions, which will be built beneath them. In the future, the terrace will become a landing pad for the flying house.

The flying house will be a mobile residence and a means of transportation at the same time.

There will be several different typologies for the flying house. Initially it will be a cabin, a modular capsule to be inserted on an aerodynamic installation that will allow it to fly. This installation will be able to unfasten the capsule and then be used as a vehicle, functioning as an individual public transportation.

Later, the flying house will be perfected and will adopt a form that integrates the capsule and the shell, in order to become a self-sufficient airplane. The issue of parking will no longer exist: if the house is a drone, it will be able to choose where landing.

acknowledgments

Some of the houses featured in this book have been published in architecture books and journals, such as *Abitare, Anfione e Zeto, Architectural Record, Domus, L'Arca International, Platform, The Plan Magazine*, and *The Plan Journal*. They have been presented in many institutions and schools of architecture, among which MAXXI Museum and MACRO Museum in Rome; the Accademia Nazionale di San Luca; Cornell University, Syracuse University, The University of Queensland, Universites of Genoa, Trento, Ascoli, Florence, Accademia di Architettura della Svizzera Italiana and Politecnico di Milano. Some of the drawings contained here have been shown in architecture and design exhibitions and in collective events.

I want to express my gratitude to all the people who supported this work, from my father, who provided structural engineering consultancy, to my colleagues Fabio and Simone Petrini who created the conditions to build these houses, from my clients to workers and manufacturers. I want to particularily thank Pippo Ciorra who accepted to write this book's presentation, Caterina Padoa Schioppa and Luca Lanini who kindly revised the book's contents, Thomas Robinson who revised the English version of this text and the Università di Pisa which supported this publication.

This work was also supported by the Università di Pisa under the "PRA - Progetti di Ricerca di Ateneo" (Institutional Research Grants) - Project no. PRA_2020-2021_41 "Resilience of small historical urban centers and transportation networks".

list of illustrations

pages 2-3
photo by Fabio Petrini
pages 6-7,8-9,10-11
photo by Fabio Bascetta
page 23
photo by Fabio Bascetta
page 25
drone photo by Gianluca Caravaggi
pages 31,33,35
photo by Yuzhen Zhang
page 37
photo by Matteo Benedetti
page 39
photo by Lina Malfona
page 41
photo by Fabio Bascetta
pages 43, 50
Photos by Fabio Petrini
page 52
photo by Matteo Benedetti
page 53
photo by Yuzhen Zhang
page 54
photo by Fabio Bascetta
page 58
photo by Lina Malfona
pages 62-63
Photo by Fabio Petrini
page 64
photos by Lina Malfona, Fabio Petrini, Yuzhen Zhang
page 74
photo by Matteo Benedetti
page 75
photo by Lina Malfona
page 84
Drawing by Raphael R. G. Maugeri, Daniele Gemini, Salvatore Porcelli, Mirco Salameh, 1-year BArch Architecture studio, Universita di Pisa, professors: Lina Malfona, Lucia Giorgetti, Giovanni Santi, Fall Semester 2020.

page 86
Drawing by Caterina Paladini, Elena Tarabella, 1-year BArch Architecture studio, Universita di Pisa, professors: Lina Malfona, Lucia Giorgetti, Giovanni Santi.
page 88
Drawings by Leonardo Bisogno Bernardini, Marco Di Mauro, 2-year MArch Architecture studio, Universita di Pisa, professors: Lina Malfona, Benedetta Marradi, Spring Semester 2020.
pages 90-91
Drawings by Marco Bonuccelli, Michele Coppede, 2-year MArch Architecture studio, Universita di Pisa, professors: Lina Malfona, Benedetta Marradi.
page 92
Drawings by Lady Lissette Cabezas Villafuerte, Allegra Freschi, 1-year BArch Architecture studio, Universita di Pisa, professors: Lina Malfona, Lucia Giorgetti, Giovanni Santi, Fall Semester 2020.
page 94
Drawing by Alessia Giuffrida, Hafsa Chafra, 1-year BArch Architecture studio, Universita di Pisa, professors: Lina Malfona, Lucia Giorgetti, Giovanni Santi.
page 96
Drawings by Gioele Storti, Niccolo Bonannini, 1-year BArch Architecture studio,

Universita di Pisa, professors: Lina Malfona, Lucia Giorgetti, Giovanni Santi.
page 97
Drawings by Lorenzo Bellè, Tommaso Vitellozzi, 1-year BArch Architecture studio, Universita di Pisa, professors: Lina Malfona, Lucia Giorgetti, Giovanni Santi.
page 108
photo by Fabio Bascetta
page 112
photo by Angelo Talia
pages 124-125
photo by Matteo Benedetti
pages 126-133
photo by Fabio Bascetta
pages 137-179
photos by Matteo Benedetti
pages 180-185
photos by Angelo Talia
pages 189-199
photos by Matteo Benedetti
page 203
photo by Fabio Bascetta
pages 204-219
photos by Matteo Benedetti
pages 220-21
photo by Fabio Bascetta

All the drawings not mentioned in this list have been made by Lina Malfona.

residentialism
a suburban archipelago

AUTHOR
Lina Malfona

PUBLISHED BY
Actar Publishers
New York, Barcelona

TEXTS
Lina Malfona

FOREWORD
Pippo Ciorra

COPY-EDITING
Angela K. Bunning

GRAPHIC DESIGN
Lina Malfona/Ramon Prat

DISTRIBUTION:
Actar Distribution Inc.

New York
440 Park Avenue South,
17th Floor
NEW YORK, NY 10016, USA
T +1 2129662207
salesnewyork@actar-d.com

Barcelona
Roca i Batlle 2-4
08023 BARCELONA, Spain
T +34 933 282 183
eurosales@actar-d.com

ISBN: 978-1-948765-84-8
PCN: Library of Congress
Control Number: 2020949076
Printed in Europe, 2021

EDITORIAL SERIES
Architecture Theory

SCIENTIFIC COMMITTE
Areti Markopoulou,
Institute of Advanced
Architecture of Catalonia (Iaac)

Elisa Cattaneo,
Politecnico di Milano

Lluís Ortega,
Illinois Institute of Technology
and ETSAVallès, Universitat
Politecnica de Catalunya

Roi Salgueiro,
Massachusetts Institute
of Technology, School of
Architecture + Planning

Ricardo Devesa,
ETSALa Salle, Universitat
Ramon Llull

This book has been supported
by Università di Pisa
under the "PRA - Progetti di
Ricerca di Ateneo" (Institutional
Research Grants) - Project no.
PRA_2020-2021_41 "Resilience
of small historical urban centers
and transportation networks".

UNIVERSITÀ DI PISA